vá

SAINT JOSEMARÍA ESCRIVÁ

Conversations with Saint Josemaría Escrivá

 Scepter

CONVERSATIONS WITH JOSEMARÍA ESCRIVÁ
Translated from *Conversaciones con Mons. Escrivá de Balaguer*

Translation, Introduction, Footnotes, and Indices are copyright ©
Fundación Studium, Madrid, and are used with permission.

To learn more about St. Josemaría Escrivá and Opus Dei,
go to www.josemariaescriva.info and www.escrivaworks.org.

First published November 1968

This edition copyright © 2007
Scepter Publishers Inc., New York
www.scepterpublishers.org
ISBN 978-1-59417-057-7
Typeset in ITC Garamond fonts

Printed in the United States of America

Contents

Foreword   7

Freedom and Pluralism in the People of God   19
Interview with Pedro Rodriguez (*Palabra*)

Why Opus Dei?   49
Interview with Peter Forbarth (*Time* magazine)

The Apostolate of Opus Dei on Five Continents   66
Interview with Jacques Guillemé-Brûlon (*Le Figaro*)

What Is the Attraction of Opus Dei?   76
Interview with Tad Szulc (*New York Times*)

Opus Dei: Fostering the Search for Holiness   87
Interview with Enrico Zuppi and Antonio Fugardi
(*L'Osservatore della Domenica*)

The University at the Service of Society   115
Interview with Andrés Garrigó (*Gaceta Universitaria*)

Women in Social Life and in Church Life   130
Interview with Pilar Salcedo (*Telva*)

Passionately Loving the World   175
*Homily given during Mass on the campus of the
University of Navarre, October 8, 1967*

Notes   187
Index of Scripture References   191
Index of Topics   193
About the Author   199

Foreword

This book gathers together the texts of interviews given by Monsignor Escrivá de Balaguer to journalists from a number of countries. It also includes the text of a homily delivered by Monsignor Escrivá at the University of Navarre (Spain) during an assembly of the Friends of the University attended by more than forty thousand people from Spain, Italy, Germany, France, Portugal, and other European countries. This homily gives a very clear and direct expression to some central aspects of the spirit which runs through all Monsignor Escrivá's answers in the various interviews.

For many people, Josemaría Escrivá's name is linked with a book, *The Way*, which has been called the "Kempis of modern times," a best-seller in the field of spiritual literature. First published in 1934 as *Consideraciones espirituales,* it has gone through 181 editions in 35 languages, with a total printing to date of more than three million copies. People of the most varied backgrounds have discovered in its counsels, full of supernatural spirit, a way to have a life of union with God in the middle of the world.

To anyone who follows the life of the Church, the name of Josemaría Escrivá immediately calls to mind that of Opus Dei, an institution which, from its foundation in 1928, came to remind Christians that "sanctity is not something for the privileged few, because all the paths of the earth can be divine." A channel was thus opened for men and women living in the world—ordinary people—effectively to seek sanctity and to carry out apostolate with a genuine and fully secular dedication and with a specifically lay spirituality.

The importance of Opus Dei as a pastoral phenomenon in the Church, as well as a sociological phenomenon, is easy to recognize today. When Monsignor Escrivá died, on June 26, 1975, Opus Dei had already spread to five continents, with a membership of more than sixty thousand people of eighty nationalities. On September 15, 1975, Monsignor Alvaro del Portillo was elected as his successor, after having been his closest collaborator for forty years. While keeping the momentum of Opus Dei's growth and holding on most faithfully to the founder's spirit, Monsignor del Portillo went on with the work—initiated by Monsignor Escrivá with the encouragement of Paul VI—of finding for Opus Dei the permanent juridical framework adapted to its foundational charism and sociological reality, rather than the juridical clothing of a secular institute, which was worn at that time by Opus Dei.

This work came to an end on November 28, 1982, when His Holiness John Paul II erected Opus Dei as a personal Prelature, just as Monsignor Escrivá had wished many years back. In short, the legal status of Opus Dei in the Church is that of a personal Prelature of worldwide scope, endowed with its own statutes and with its central seat at Rome.

The present volume gathers from the lips of its founder several explanations of what Opus Dei is, as well as a number of descriptions of the basic aspects of its juridical status and organization. These statements can be fully grasped only if one bears in mind what was mentioned above, namely, that Opus Dei at that time found itself in a temporary juridical situation, and so Monsignor Escrivá could not use—even though at times he hinted at it—the terminology adapted to the definitive juridical framework, which he had foreseen but which had not yet been arrived at. Specifically, throughout this volume the reader will find terms such as "Association" referring to Opus Dei, and "President General" referring to the Prelate. For this reason it has been thought appropriate, besides the present explanations, to add some brief explanatory notes to the text.

It should be pointed out that the difficulty of having to use an inadequate juridical terminology is overcome by the "gift of tongues" of Monsignor Escrivá. The reader can therefore draw from his answers—aside from many clear criteria regarding current issues in the life of the Church and of society—a broad and deep knowledge of the spiritual, pastoral, and juridical reality of Opus Dei. Nevertheless, the reading will be even more profitable if one has a previous knowledge of the present juridical status of this institution, to which there are implicit allusions in some of Monsignor Escrivá's answers. This is the reason for the following paragraphs.

Since its erection as a personal Prelature, Opus Dei is composed of a Prelate, who is its own Ordinary; of the clergy or presbytery of the Prelature, who are the priests incardinated in Opus Dei; and of the lay people who have been freely incorporated or will be in the future.

The priests come exclusively from the ranks of the laymen of Opus Dei, and they receive Holy Orders after having completed the required ecclesiastical studies. No priests or candidates for the priesthood are therefore taken from any diocese. The lay people of the Prelature are men and women, single or married, of every race and sector of society, without any restriction for reasons of health, age, family situation, professional status, or any similar circumstance.

For all the faithful belonging to Opus Dei—whether they are clerics or lay people—the calling is one and the same, viz., a definite vocation whereby, in a manner suited to their various circumstances and personal situations, they take up the same ascetical and formative commitments, and all the members of the Prelature have a full share in the special apostolate carried out by Opus Dei.

The Opus Dei Prelature—which constitutes a pastoral unit both organic and indivisible—carries out its apostolic action through both the Men's Section and the Women's Section under the government and direction of the Prelate—who provides and assures the fundamental unity of spirit and jurisdiction of both Sections—and of his Vicars with the pastoral assistance of the Prelature's clergy.

The Prelate, who is the Ordinary of the Opus Dei Prelature, governs both Sections, helped by his councils, which are distinct for each Section. In each country there are similar councils to assist the Regional Vicar in his work of government.

The Prelate has an ordinary power of government or jurisdiction, limited to whatever refers to the specific aim of the Prelature. This area of his jurisdiction differs substantially, on account of its matter, from the jurisdiction of diocesan bishops for the ordinary pastoral care of the faithful. Aside from governing his own clergy, the Prelate's jurisdiction includes the general direction of the training and specific spiritual and apostolic attention received by the lay people incorporated to Opus Dei with a view to a more intense dedication to the service of the Church.

The lay members are under the jurisdiction of the Prelate in whatever refers to the fulfillment of the special commitments—ascetical, formative, and apostolic—which they freely make by means of the bond of dedication to the Prelature's specific aim.

The faithful of the Opus Dei Prelature are people who wish to lead a fully Christian life, seeking sanctity and doing apostolate in their own state in life and in their work in the midst of secular society. The incorporation to Opus Dei is made by means of a bond of a contractual character, mutual and stable, between the Prelature and the lay faithful who freely wish to be incorporated.

The Prelature commits itself to supply its faithful with a regular doctrinal-religious, spiritual, ascetical, and apostolic training, as well as with the required specific pastoral attention from the Opus Dei clergy.

For their part, the Opus Dei faithful bind themselves to put into practice the ascetical, formative, and apostolic commitments specified in the Prelature's own statutes; to fulfill the disciplinary norms regulating Opus Dei's life; and to support themselves—and support their own family, if that is the case—by means of their own professional work, through which they will also contribute, according to their ability, to support the formative and apostolic undertakings of the Prelature.

In Opus Dei there is the same variety of faithful as in all other jurisdictional structures of a secular character—a diocese, for example; namely, priests and lay people, men and women, young and elderly, single and married, people of any social condition and of any honest trade or profession.

Upon incorporation to Opus Dei the faithful take up specific commitments—ascetical, formative, apostolic, and disciplinary—defined by precise juridical norms which are spelled out in the statutes of the Prelature. These commitments bring with them a special and full personal dedication to the service of the apostolic mission of the Church, each one within his or her own state in life, and within the canonical condition of ordinary secular faithful—whether they are clerics or lay people—which is not changed by the incorporation to Opus Dei.

The purpose of the Opus Dei Prelature has a twofold apostolic or pastoral dimension. On one hand, the Prelate—together with his clergy—carries out a special pastoral work by attending to and sustaining the faithful incorporated to Opus Dei in the fulfillment of the ascetical, formative, and apostolic commitments they have made, which are quite demanding. On the other, the Prelature—both clergy and laity, jointly and inseparably united—carries out the specific apostolate of spreading a deep awareness of the universal call to holiness and apostolate in all environments of society and, more specifically, of the sanctifying value of ordinary professional work.

Furthermore, some members of Opus Dei, together with many other people—including non-Catholics—give rise in all parts of the world to all sorts of apostolic undertakings, moved by their love for the Church. In some cases Opus Dei as an institution lends them a specific pastoral assistance by assuring a suitable spiritual attention for the beneficiaries of those undertakings who freely wish to avail themselves of it. These undertakings are always apostolic in their aim and are conducted in a professional and secular manner.

In addition, the Priestly Society of the Holy Cross is intrinsically and indissolubly joined to the Opus Dei Prelature, and its aim is to spread the foundational charism of Opus Dei among the secular clergy.

The Prelate of Opus Dei is concurrently president general of the Priestly Society of the Holy Cross. All the priests incardinated in the Prelature are *ipso iure* members of this Association. Other secular priests may be admitted as members while remaining incardinated in their respective dioceses and under the exclusive jurisdiction of their own bishop, who is their only superior.

The Priestly Society of the Holy Cross is therefore an association whose purpose is to foster priestly holiness in the practice of the priestly ministry. Associations of this type were praised and encouraged by the Second Vatican Council in its Decree on priests. To this effect, the Priestly Society of the Holy Cross supplies its members with suitable spiritual and ascetical attention, which leads them, among other things, to give a good example of availability to their Ordinaries' requirements and diocesan needs.

* * *

The development of Opus Dei and the influence of its spirit and its apostolates in the life of the Church account for the interest it has aroused in public opinion. This interest has led many journalists to put specific questions to Monsignor Escrivá de Balaguer on subjects of particular concern to their readers; these he has answered in writing and at length.

Pedro Rodriguez, editor of the theological monthly *Palabra* (Madrid), interviewed Monsignor Escrivá de Balaguer (then a doctor of theology and member of the Roman Academy of Theology) to obtain his authoritative opinion on some of the major problems facing the Church today. Among the subjects he covers are postconciliar Catholicism, the apostolate of lay people, the presence of priests among their fellow men, and the Christianizing of earthly realities. This interview also indicates the role of Opus Dei in the Church and in the world and touches on some aspects of its spirit. A recurring note in this long conversation is Monsignor Escrivá's sense of the Church, which helps him to grasp the real needs of the moment and to approach them in an apostolic way. Closely united to this attitude is his appreciation of pluralism, which stems not only from respect for the rights and freedom of the Church but also from faith in the action of God, who guides it, endowing it with an inexhaustible variety of gifts and charisms.

The ideas contained in this first interview offer a framework for the more specific questions of the three conversations which follow—with Peter Forbarth of *Time*, Jacques Guillemé-Brûlon of *Le Figaro*, and Tad Szulc of the *New York Times*. These three journalists had in mind the millions of readers of these newspapers in the United States and France; the subjects are dealt with against a background of current affairs, often referring to people and events in international political life, which can offer the public a familiar setting for approaching deeper questions of a spiritual and apostolic nature or even matters dealing specifically with theology or canon law.

The interview with *Le Figaro* was published on May 16, 1966, and is therefore the first in order of time of those included in this book; those with Peter Forbarth and Tad Szulc are previously unpublished: they were used as background material for a variety of articles.

Opus Dei's spirit and apostolate are also the central theme of the interview Monsignor Escrivá de Balaguer gave to *L'Osservatore della Domenica*. In this Vatican weekly, the position of the Church today forms the central topic of a lengthy conversation with Enrico Zuppi, the editor, and Antonio Fugardi, a staff journalist.

Another interview deals with the specialized subject of the university. Here Monsignor Escrivá de Balaguer expresses not only his apostolic viewpoint as founder of Opus Dei but also his personal opinions on a subject which has always interested him and to which he has made a very substantial contribution both personally—he is a consultor of the Sacred Congregation for Seminaries and Universities—and through the activity of the members of Opus Dei. One of his first apostolic activities was precisely his involvement in Ferraz Residence Hall in Madrid, during the second Spanish Republic. This was a university hall designed as a contribution to university teaching to foster a broader formation of students; since then, this type of educational institution has spread considerably in a great variety of countries. Another activity in the educational field which is of great importance is the University of Navarre, of which Monsignor Escrivá de Balaguer is chancellor; begun in 1952, this university in the north of Spain has achieved worldwide recognition in certain subjects. Because of its residential structure, its attempt to combine the Anglo-Saxon tradition with the Latin, the high scientific standards of its teaching and research, and the international character of its student body and teaching staff, the University of Navarre has made a valuable contribution to education. Knowing Monsignor Escrivá de Balaguer's interest in education, Andrés Garrigó, editor of the student magazine *Gaceta Universitaria* (Madrid), put to him a series of questions that make up this interview.

The last interview, with Pilar Salcedo, editor of *Telva* (Madrid), one of the better-known Spanish language magazines for women, deals in a concise and often humorous way with the problems that contemporary society poses for women and the family. Its definite and warm words cover not only the principles of family sociology but also topics such as home life and the active participation of women in public life and in the fullness of the life of the Church.

Taking into account the aforementioned clarifications regarding the different juridical situation of Opus Dei at the time Monsignor Escrivá granted these interviews, the whole set of texts gathered in this book provides a broad view of some aspects of the spirit, structure, and apostolic aim of Opus Dei, as well as characteristic features of its founder's personality.

Readers will detect two constant characteristics in the words of Monsignor Escrivá: supernatural spirit and human warmth. We wish therefore to finish this introduction by underlining a central idea of these "conversations" with the founder of Opus Dei: his love for freedom, expressed in the conviction with which he defends the ideas he believes in while keeping an inexhaustible capacity for understanding and living in harmony with people who may differ from him.

Conversations with Saint Josemaría Escrivá

Freedom and Pluralism in the People of God

Interview with Pedro Rodriguez (*Palabra*)
—published October 1967

We would like to begin this interview with a subject on which opinions are highly divided: the question of aggiornamento. *In your opinion, what is the real meaning of this word in the life of the Church?*

Faithfulness. Aggiornamento, as I see it, means above all 1
faithfulness. A husband, a soldier, an administrator, who faithfully fulfills at each moment, in each new circumstance of his life, the duties of love and justice which he once took on, will always be just that much better a husband, soldier, or administrator. It is difficult to keep this keen sense of loyalty constantly active, as it is always difficult to apply a principle to the changing realities of the contingent world. But it is the best defense against ageing of the spirit, hardening of the heart, and stiffening of the mind.

The same applies to the lives of institutions and, in a very special way, to the life of the Church, which does not follow a precarious human plan but a God-given design. The world's redemption and salvation are the fruit of Jesus Christ's loving filial faithfulness to the will of the heavenly Father who sent him, and of our faithfulness to him. Therefore, *aggiornamento* in the Church, today as in any other period, is fundamentally a joyful reaffirmation of the People of God's faithfulness to the mission received, to the gospel.

This faithfulness should be alive and active in every circumstance of men's lives. It therefore requires opportune doctrinal developments in the exposition of the riches of the *depositum fidei*, as can clearly be seen in the two thousand years of the Church's history and recently in the Second Vatican Council. It may also require suitable changes and reforms to improve, in their human and perfectible element, the organizational structures and the missionary and apostolic methods of the Church. But it would be, to say the least, superficial to think that *aggiornamento* consists primarily in change, or that all change produces *aggiornamento*. One need only consider that there are people who seek changes which go outside and against the Council's doctrine and would put the progressive movement of the People of God back several centuries in history, back at least to feudal times.

The Second Vatican Council has often used the expression "People of God" to designate the Church. It has thus clearly shown the common responsibility of all Christians in the single mission of this People of God. What, in your opinion, should be the characteristics of the "necessary public opinion in the Church," of which Pius XII already spoke, in order to reflect effectively this common responsibility? How is the phenomenon of "public opinion in the Church" affected by the particular relationships of authority and obedience which exist in the heart of the Christian community?

2   I do not think there can be such a thing as truly Christian obedience unless that obedience is voluntary and responsible. The children of God are not stones. Nor are they corpses. They are intelligent and free beings. And all of them have been raised to the same supernatural order as those who hold authority. But no one can use his intelligence and freedom properly, whether it be to obey or to give an opinion, unless he has acquired an adequate Christian education.

The problem of "necessary public opinion in the Church" is fundamentally the same as the problem of the doctrinal training of the faithful. Certainly the Holy Spirit distributes his abundant gifts among the members of the People of God, all of whom are responsible for the mission of the Church. But far from exempting anyone from the obligation of acquiring adequate doctrinal training his action makes it more pressing.

By doctrine I mean the knowledge which each person should have of the mission of the Church as a whole and of his particular role, his specific responsibilities, in that mission. This, as the Holy Father has frequently reminded us, is the colossal task of education which the Church must undertake in the postconciliar period. The solution to the problem which you mention, as well as to other yearnings which are felt today in the heart of the Church, depends directly, I feel, on how well this task is done. Certainly, more or less *prophetic* intuitions of some uninstructed *charismatics* cannot guarantee the necessary public opinion among the People of God.

Regarding the forms of expression of this public opinion, I don't think it is a question of organs and institutions. A diocesan pastoral council, the columns of a newspaper, even though it isn't officially Catholic, or even a personal letter from one of the faithful to his bishop can all be equally effective. There are many legitimate ways in which the faithful can express their opinion. They neither can nor should be *straitjacketed* by creating a new body or institution. And much less if it meant having an institution which ran the risk of being monopolized or made use of, as could so easily happen, by a group or clique of official Catholics, regardless of their tendencies or orientation. That would endanger the prestige of the hierarchy itself, and it would seem a mockery to the other members of the People of God.

The concept of "People of God," to which we referred before, expresses the historical character of the Church as a reality of divine origin which also includes some changing and transitory elements. Bearing this in mind, how should the priestly character be expressed in the lives of priests today? What aspects of the priest's life, as described in the Decree Presbyterorum ordinis, *would you underline for the present times?*

3   I would underline a characteristic of priestly existence which is not part of these changing and transitory elements. I refer to the perfect union which should exist, as the Decree *Presbyterorum ordinis* reminds us on several occasions, between a priest's consecration and his mission. Or, in other words, between his personal life of piety and the exercise of his priestly ministry; between his filial relationship with God, and his pastoral and brotherly relations with men. I do not believe a priest can carry out an effective ministry unless he is a man of prayer.

Some sectors of the clergy are concerned about the presence of the priest in society. Taking their cue from the Council (Constitution Lumen gentium, *no. 31; Decree* Presbyterorum ordinis, *no. 8), they propose that priests undertake a professional or manual activity in civil life: "priests in the factory," for example. We would like to know your opinion on this.*

4   Let me first say that even though I consider it mistaken for many reasons, I respect the opinion contrary to my own, and recognize the apostolic zeal of its proponents, who can count on my prayers and affection.

A priest's ministry may be encumbered by timidity and *complexes*, which usually indicate human immaturity, or by *clerical* tendencies, which denote supernatural immaturity. But when the priesthood is properly exercised, without those obstacles, I think it is sufficient in itself to ensure a legitimate, simple, and authentic presence of the priest-man among the other members of the human community to whom he addresses himself. Usually nothing more will be needed in order to be in living communion with the world of work, to understand its problems and to share its fortunes. Recourse to the ingenuous "passport" of "amateur lay" activities can offend for all sorts of reasons the average layman's good sense and will rarely be effective, because its very lack of authenticity condemns it to failure from the outset.

The priestly ministry, especially in these times of great scarcity of clergy, is a terribly absorbing task which leaves no time for "double-jobbing." Men need us so much (though many do not realize it) that there will never be a surplus of priests. We need more helping hands, more time, more energy. This is why I often say to my sons who are priests that the day one of them noticed that he had time on his hands, he could be quite sure he had not lived his priesthood well that day.

And bear in mind that in the case of these priests of Opus Dei, we are dealing with men who before receiving Holy Orders usually have worked for years in some intellectual or manual activity in civil life. They are priest-engineers, priest-doctors, priest-workers, and so on. Nevertheless, as far as I know, none of them has thought it necessary to approach men with a slide-rule, a stethoscope, or a pneumatic drill in order to make himself heard or to win the esteem of civil society and his former colleagues and companions. It is true that at times they exercise their professions or trades, in a way compatible with the obligations of the clerical state. But they never feel impelled to do so in order to be "present in civil life." Their motives are different: social charity, for example, or absolute financial need, in order to initiate some apostolic undertaking. Saint Paul too had occasion to return to his trade as a tent-maker. But not because Ananias told him in Damascus that he should learn to make tents in order to be able to preach Christ's gospel to the Gentiles in a fitting manner.

To sum up—and may I make it clear that with this I am not prejudging the legitimacy or the rectitude of intention of any apostolic activity—I see the professional man or the worker who becomes a priest as more authentic and more in accordance with the doctrine of Vatican II than the figure of the worker-priest. Except in the field of specialized pastoral work, which will always be necessary, the "classical" figure of the worker-priest already belongs to the past: a past in which the marvelous potential of the lay apostolate was hidden to many eyes.

At times we hear complaints about priests who adopt definite positions on temporal problems and particularly on political questions. Today, unlike other times, many of these positions are taken up to favor greater freedom, social justice, and so on. Undoubtedly, active intervention in these matters is not proper to the ministerial priesthood, apart from exceptional cases; but do you not think that a priest should denounce injustice, the absence of freedom, and so on, as un-Christian? How can these opposing demands be reconciled?

5   A priest, by virtue of his teaching mission, should preach all the Christian virtues and their practical demands and manifestations in the concrete circumstances of the lives of the men to whom he ministers. He should, also, teach men to respect and esteem the dignity and freedom with which God has endowed the human person, and the special supernatural dignity which a Christian receives at Baptism.

No priest who fulfills this duty of his ministry can ever be accused, except through ignorance or bad faith, of *meddling in politics*. Nor could it be said that his teaching interferes in the apostolic task, which belongs specifically to the laity, of ordering temporal structures and occupations in a Christian fashion.

Concern is felt throughout the Church for the problems of the Third World. It is generally recognized that one of the great difficulties derives from the shortage of clergy, and particularly of native priests. What is your opinion, and what experience have you had in this field?

I fully agree that the increase in native clergy is a problem of   6 primary importance for ensuring not only the development but even the permanence of the Church in many countries, especially in those which are undergoing a period of bitter nationalism.

As regards my own experience in this field, I must say it is one of the many motives I have for giving thanks to our Lord. Hundreds of laymen of Opus Dei from more than sixty nations, including many where the Church urgently needs to develop a native clergy, are being trained and ordained priests with sound doctrine, a universal (catholic) outlook, and an ardent spirit of service. (I can say that they are certainly better than I am.) Some have been consecrated bishops in countries where the problem is particularly acute and have already established flourishing seminaries.

Priests are incardinated in a diocese and depend on the Ordinary. What justification can there be for them to belong to an association which is distinct from the diocese and even organized on a worldwide basis?

7   The justification is clear: legitimate use of the natural right of association, which the Church recognizes for the clergy as well as for the rest of the faithful. There is a centuries-old tradition testified to by the example of the many praiseworthy associations which have helped the spiritual life of secular priests. It has been repeatedly reaffirmed in the teaching of the recent popes (Pius XII, John XXIII, and Paul VI), and in the solemn declarations of the Second Vatican Council (see Decree *Presbyterorum ordinis*, no. 8).

It is worth bearing in mind here that the competent conciliar Commission rejected, with the subsequent approval of the General Congregation, a Council father's proposal that there be no sacerdotal associations other than those fostered or directed by the diocesan bishop. It clearly based its rejection on the natural right of association, which the clergy also enjoy; the reply went: "What the Council has declared as befitting lay people (in that it derives from natural law and suits the dignity of human nature) cannot be denied to priests." [1]

By virtue of this fundamental right, priests are free to found associations or to become members of those which already exist, provided the associations pursue good aims which are in keeping with the dignity and requirements of the clerical state. To understand properly the legitimacy and scope of the secular clergy's right of association and avoid all misunderstandings, reservations, or danger of anarchy, one should recall the distinction which necessarily exists and which should be respected between the cleric's ministerial function and the sphere of his personal life.

8   In fact a cleric and, particularly, a priest, incorporated by the sacrament of Holy Orders into the Ordo Presbyterorum, is constituted by divine law as a cooperator of the Episcopal Order. The specific ministerial function of diocesan priests is determined, according to the practice of ecclesiastical law, by

incardination, which attaches a priest to the service of a local church, under the authority of the respective bishop, and by a canonical mission, which confers upon a priest a definite ministry within the unity of the Presbyterium, whose head is the bishop. It is obvious, therefore, that the priest depends on his bishop, by virtue of a sacramental and juridical bond, in everything which refers to the assignment of his particular pastoral work; the doctrinal and disciplinary instructions which he receives for the exercise of his ministry; a just financial remuneration; and in all the pastoral indications which the bishop may give for the care of souls, for divine worship, and for applying the prescriptions of common law relating to the rights and obligations derived from the clerical state.

All these necessary relations of dependence give juridical expression to the pastoral obedience, unity, and communion with his own Ordinary, which a priest ought to live with tact and refinement. But there also exists in the life of a secular priest a legitimate sphere of personal autonomy, freedom, and responsibility, in which he enjoys the same rights and obligations as any other person in the Church. His juridical condition is thus clearly different from that of minors (of canon 89 of the Code of Canon Law) and from that of the religious, who renounce the exercise of all or some of their personal rights by virtue of their religious profession.

Within the general limits of morality and of the duties proper to his state, a secular priest can freely administer and decide, individually or together with others in an association, all the spiritual, cultural, and financial aspects of his personal life. He is free to look after his own cultural development in accordance with his personal preferences and capabilities. He is free to lead the social life he wishes, and order his life as he thinks best, provided that he fulfils the obligations of his ministry. He is free to dispose of his personal private goods according to the dictates of his conscience. And, above all, he is free in his spiritual and ascetic life and in his acts of piety to follow the inspirations of the Holy Spirit and to choose, from among the many means which the Church counsels or permits, those which are most suited to his own particular circumstances.

Both the Second Vatican Council and Pope Paul VI in his encyclical *Sacerdotalis coelibatus* have earnestly commended diocesan and interdiocesan, national, and worldwide associations which foster the holiness of priests in the exercise of their ministry and have been approved by the appropriate ecclesiastical authorities. The existence of such associations in no way weakens, as I have already said, the bond of communion and dependence which links each priest with his bishop, the brotherly unity which unites the members of the priesthood, nor the effectiveness of each priest's service in his own local Church.

The mission of the laity is carried out, according to the Council, in the Church and in the world. Often this is misunderstood because people concentrate on one aspect or the other. How would you explain the laity's task in the Church and in the world?

9   I think by no means should they be considered two different tasks. The layman's specific role in the mission of the Church is precisely that of sanctifying secular reality, the temporal order, the world, *ab intra*, in an immediate and direct way.

In addition to his secular task, a layman (like a cleric or a religious) has certain fundamental rights, duties, and powers within ecclesiastical society related to his juridical status as a member of the faithful: active participation in the liturgy, the possibility of cooperating directly in the hierarchy's apostolate, and of offering advice to the hierarchy in its pastoral task if invited to do so, and so forth.

The specific task which belongs to the layman as *layman* and his generic or common one as a *member of the faithful* are not opposed but rather superimposed. They are not contradictory but complementary. To concentrate solely on the specific secular mission of the layman and to forget his membership in the Church would be as absurd as to imagine a green branch in full bloom which did not belong to any tree. But to forget what is specific and proper to the layman, or to misunderstand the characteristics of his apostolic tasks and their value to the Church, would be to reduce the flourishing tree of the Church to the monstrous condition of a barren trunk.

You have been saying and writing for many years that the vocation of the laity consists in three things: "to sanctify work, to sanctify themselves in work, and to sanctify others through work." Could you explain exactly what you mean by sanctifying work?

It is difficult to explain it in a few words, because the expression "sanctifying work" involves fundamental concepts of the theology of Creation. What I have always taught, over the last forty years, is that a Christian should do all honest human work, be it intellectual or manual, with the greatest perfection possible: with human perfection (professional competence) and with Christian perfection (for love of God's will and as a service to mankind). Human work done in this manner, no matter how humble or insignificant it may seem, helps to shape the world in a Christian way. The world's divine dimension is made more visible and our human labor is thus incorporated into the marvelous work of Creation and Redemption. It is raised to the order of grace. It is sanctified and becomes God's work, *operatio Dei, opus Dei.*

We have reminded Christians of the wonderful words of

Genesis which tell us that God created man so that he might work, and have concentrated on the example of Christ, who spent most of his life on earth working as a craftsman in a village. We love human work, which he chose as his state in life and which he cultivated and sanctified. We see in work, in men's noble creative toil, not only one of the highest human values, an indispensable means to social progress and to greater justice in the relations between men, but also a sign of God's love for his creatures and of men's love for each other and for God: we see in work a means of perfection, a way to sanctity.

Hence, the sole objective of Opus Dei has always been to see that there be men and women of all races and social conditions who endeavor to love and to serve God and the rest of mankind in and through their ordinary work, in the midst of the realities and interests of the world.

The Decree Apostolicam actuositatem, *no. 5, clearly affirms that it is the mission of the whole Church to instill a Christian spirit in the temporal order. This mission therefore pertains to everyone: hierarchy, clergy, religious, and laity. Could you tell us how you see the role and function of each of these sectors in the Church in this single common mission?*

11   You will find, in fact, that the answer is given in the Council documents. The role of the hierarchy is to point out, as part of its Magisterium, the doctrinal principles which must preside over and illuminate the carrying out of this apostolic task (see Constitution *Lumen gentium*, no. 28; Constitution *Gaudium et spes*, no. 43; Decree *Apostolicam actuositatem*, no. 24).

The *immediate* task of directly ordering temporal realities in the light of the doctrinal principles enunciated by the

Magisterium corresponds specifically to the laity, who work immersed in all the circumstances and structures of secular life. But, at the same time, they must act with the necessary personal autonomy in taking concrete decisions in their social, family, political, and cultural life (see *Lumen gentium*, no. 31; *Gaudium et spes*, no. 43; *Apostolicam actuositatem*, no. 7).

The mission of religious, who separate themselves from secular realities and activities to take up a particular state of life, is to give public, eschatological witness, which helps to remind the rest of the faithful that the earth is not their permanent home (see *Lumen gentium*, no. 44; Decree *Perfectae caritatis*, no. 5). The numerous works of charity and social welfare which so many religious men and women carry out with a great spirit of self-sacrifice also constitute a contribution toward instilling Christian spirit into the temporal order.

One characteristic of all Christian life, no matter what form it takes, is the "dignity and freedom of the children of God." Throughout your teaching, you have insistently defended the freedom of the laity. To what exactly do you refer?

I refer precisely to the personal freedom of every layman to   12
take, in the light of principles given by the Church, all the concrete theoretical or practical decisions which he considers most appropriate and most in agreement with his own personal convictions and aptitudes. For example, decisions referring to different philosophical or political views, to different artistic or cultural trends, or to the problems of professional and social life.

All those who exercise the priestly ministry in the Church should always be careful to respect the autonomy which a

Catholic layman needs, so that he will not find himself in a position of inferiority in relation to his fellow laymen and can efficiently carry out his own apostolic task in the middle of the world. To attempt the opposite, to try to *instrumentalize* lay people for ends which exceed the proper limits of our hierarchical ministry, would be to fall into a lamentably anachronistic clericalism. The possibilities of the lay apostolate would be terribly curtailed; the laity would be condemned to permanent immaturity; and, above all, today especially, the very concept of authority and unity in the Church would be endangered. We cannot forget that the existence among Catholics of a true diversity of criterion and opinion in matters which God has left to the free discussion of men is in no way opposed to the hierarchical structure or the unity of the People of God. On the contrary, it strengthens them and defends them against possible impurities.

The vocation of the laity and that of religious—though they share a common Christian vocation—are very different. How is it possible, then, for religious to prepare students in their schools for their vocation as lay people?

13   It is possible insofar as religious, whose meritorious work in the service of the Church I sincerely admire, attempt to understand fully the characteristics and demands of the lay vocation to holiness and apostolate in the middle of the world, and insofar as they respect them and know how to teach them to the students.

Not infrequently, in speaking of the laity, people tend to ignore women, and thus they give a confused picture of the role of women in the Church. Similarly, people tend to understand the social emancipation of women simply as the participation of women in public life. What do you think is the mission of women in the Church and in the world?

To begin with, I see no reason why one should make any   14
distinction or discrimination with respect to women when
speaking of the laity and its apostolic task, its rights and
duties. All the baptized, men and women alike, share equally
in the dignity, freedom, and responsibility of the children of
God. There exists in the Church that fundamental unity
which Saint Paul taught to the first Christians: *Quicumque
enim in Christo baptizati estis, Christum induistis. Non est
Iudaeus, neque Graecus: non est servus, neque liber: non
est masculus, neque femina* ["Now there is no distinction
between Jew and Greek, nor between slave and freeman, nor
between man and woman"] (Gal 3: 2-28).

For many reasons, including some derived from divine
positive law, I consider that the distinction between men
and women with respect to the juridical capacity for receiving Holy Orders should be retained. But in all other spheres I
think the Church should fully recognize in her legislation,
internal life, and apostolic action exactly the same rights
and duties for women as for men. For example, the right to
do apostolate, to found and direct associations, to give their
opinion responsibly on matters which affect the common
good of the Church. I fully realize that all this, which is not
difficult to admit in theory when we consider the theological
arguments in favor, will in fact meet with resistance from
some quarters. I still remember the surprise and even the
criticism with which some people reacted to the idea of
Opus Dei's encouraging women who belong to our Association to seek degrees in theological studies. Now instead they
are tending to imitate us in this, as in other things.

Nevertheless, I think resistance and misgivings will dis-
appear little by little. Basically it is only a question of

understanding the Church, of realizing that the Church is not composed only of clerics and religious but that the laity also, men and women, are People of God and have by divine law a mission and responsibility of their own.

But I would like to add that, as I see it, the essential equality between men and women demands an understanding of the complementary roles which they play in the Church's growth and in the progress of society. Not in vain did God make them man and woman. This diversity should be considered not in a "patriarchal" sense but in its full rich depth of tones and consequences. In this way men are freed from the temptation of "masculinizing" the Church and society, and women from seeing their mission in the People of God and in the world as no more than showing that they can do equally well the tasks which were formerly reserved to men. I think that both men and women should rightly consider themselves as the protagonists in the history of salvation, but each complementing the work of the other.

It has been pointed out that The Way, *published in its original form in 1934, contains many ideas which were then considered "heretical" by some people and have now been confirmed in the Second Vatican Council. What can you say about this? Which are these ideas?*

15   Perhaps, if you will permit me, we can discuss this question more fully on another occasion. For the moment I would simply say that I thank our Lord for seeing fit to use *The Way*, which has run through numerous editions in many languages (the number of copies published has already passed the two and a half million mark), to place in the minds and in the lives of people of so many different races and tongues those Christian truths which were to be confirmed in the Second Vatican

Council, thus bringing peace and happiness to millions of Christians and non-Christians.

For many years you have been particularly concerned about the spiritual and human welfare of priests, and especially of diocesan priests. For as long as you could, you spent a lot of your time preaching retreats to priests and giving them spiritual guidance. At a certain point you started looking for ways in which priests who felt they had this vocation could belong to Opus Dei, while remaining fully diocesan and dependent on their Ordinaries. What circumstances in the life of the Church, apart from other reasons, motivated this concern of yours? Could you tell us in what way that activity has helped and can help to resolve some problems of the diocesan clergy or of the life of the Church?

What gave rise to my concern and to this apostolate of the   16
Work were not circumstances of a more or less accidental or transitory character, but permanent spiritual and human needs of a spiritual and human nature, intimately related to the life and work of diocesan priests. I refer fundamentally to their need of being helped to find personal holiness in the exercise of their own ministry, with a spirit and means which in no way modify their status as diocesan priests. In this way they are in a position to respond to the grace of the divine vocation which they have received with a youthful spirit and ever increasing generosity. They are able to forestall, prudently and promptly, the spiritual and human crises which can easily arise from many different factors. These possible crises may be due to isolation, environmental difficulties, indifference, the apparent futility of their work, routine, fatigue, carelessness in maintaining and perfecting their intellectual formation, and also—and this is the root cause of

crises of obedience and unity—lack of supernatural outlook in their relations with their own Ordinary and even with their brothers in the priesthood.

The diocesan priests who make legitimate use of the right of association to become members of the Sacerdotal Society of the Holy Cross [1] (Opus Dei) do so solely because they desire to receive personal spiritual help. They act in a manner entirely compatible with the duties of their state. Otherwise this help would be no help, but rather complication, hindrance, and disorder.

An essential characteristic of the spirit of Opus Dei is that it does not take anyone out of his place, *unusquisque, in qua vocatione vocatus est, in ea permaneat* (1 Cor 7: 20). Rather, it leads each person to fulfill the tasks and duties of his own state, of his mission in the Church and in society, with the greatest possible perfection. Therefore, when a priest joins the Work he neither modifies nor abandons any part of his diocesan vocation. His dedication to the service of the local Church in which he is incardinated; his full dependence on his own Ordinary, his secular spirituality, his solidarity with other priests, and so forth, are not changed. On the contrary, he undertakes to live his vocation to the full, because he knows that he must seek perfection precisely in the exercise of his obligations as a diocesan priest. In our Association this principle has a series of practical applications of a juridical and ascetic nature which it would take a long time to describe. Let me say only, by way of example, that in Opus Dei, unlike other associations where a vow or promise of obedience to the internal Superior is required, the dependence of the diocesan priests is not a dependence of government but rather a voluntary relationship of spiritual assistance. There is no internal hierarchy for them, and therefore no danger of a double bond of obedience.

What these priests find in Opus Dei is, above all, the permanent, continuous ascetical help which they want to receive, with a secular and diocesan spirituality, and independent of the personal and circumstantial changes which may take place in the government of the respective local Church. Thus, in addition to the general spiritual direction which the bishop gives with his preaching, pastoral letters, conversations, disciplinary instructions, and so on, they have a personal spiritual guidance which continues no matter where they are, and which complements the common guidance imparted by the bishop, while always, as a grave duty, giving it full respect. This personal spiritual direction, so strongly recommended by the Second Vatican Council and by the ordinary Magisterium, helps to foster the priest's life of piety, his pastoral charity, his steady continued doctrinal training, his zeal for the diocesan apostolates, his love and obedience for his own bishop, his concern for vocations to the priesthood and to the seminary, and so on.

The fruits of this work are for the local Churches where the priests serve. My soul of a diocesan priest rejoices at this. Moreover, on repeated occasions, I have had the consolation of seeing with what affection the Pope and the bishops bless, desire, and encourage this work.

On several occasions, with reference to the early years in the life of Opus Dei, you have said that all you had was "youth, the grace of God, and good humor." Besides, during the 1920s, the doctrine on the laity was not as developed as we see it today. Nevertheless, Opus Dei is now a noteworthy factor in the life of the Church. Could you explain to us how, being a young priest, you were able to have sufficient foresight and understanding to carry out this task?

I never had any other aim than that of fulfilling the will   17
of God. Please do not ask me to go into details about the

beginnings of the Work, which the Love of God began to make me suspect back in 1917. They are intimately connected with the history of my soul and belong to my interior life. All I can say is that I acted at every moment with the permission and affectionate blessing of the bishop of Madrid, who was my very dear friend and in whose diocese Opus Dei was born on October 2, 1928. And later, with the constant approval and encouragement of the Holy See and in each individual case with that of the Ordinaries of the places in which we work.

Some people, precisely because of the presence of laymen of Opus Dei in influential positions in Spanish society, speak of the influence of Opus Dei in Spain. Can you explain what this influence is?

18   I intensely dislike anything that might sound like blowing one's own trumpet. But I think it would not be humility but blindness and ingratitude to the Lord, who so generously blesses our work, if we did not recognize that Opus Dei has a real influence on the life of Spain. It is logical that in those countries where we have been working for quite a few years—and the Work has been in Spain for thirty-nine years, because it was God's will that our Association should be born to the life of the Church in Spain—the influence of Opus Dei should already have a noticeable social impact which reflects the progressive development of our apostolate.

How is this influence felt? Obviously, since Opus Dei is an Association with spiritual and apostolic aims, the nature of its influence—in Spain as in the other countries, spread over the five continents, in which we are working—can be none other than spiritual and apostolic. Opus Dei's influence in civil society is not of a temporal nature (social, political, or economic), though it is reflected in the ethical aspects of human activities. Like the influence of the Church itself, the soul of the world, it belongs to a different and higher order and is expressed precisely by the word "sanctification."

This leads us to the subject of the members of Opus Dei whom you call influential. In an association whose aim is political, those members will be *influential* who occupy positions in parliament or in government, in the council of ministers, in the cabinet. In a cultural association, the *influential* members will be philosophers of renown, or authors of national reputation, for example. But if, as in the case with Opus Dei, the Association aims at the sanctification of men's ordinary work, be it manual or intellectual, it is obvious that all its members have to be considered influential because all of them work, and in Opus Dei the general duty of man to work carries with it special disciplinary and ascetical significance. All of them endeavor to do their work, whatever it may be, in a holy, Christian manner, with a desire for perfection. For me, therefore, the witness which a son of mine who is a miner gives among his companions is as *influential*, as important and necessary, as that of a vice-chancellor of a university among the other members of the academic body.

Where, then, lies the influence of Opus Dei? The answer is easily found when we consider the sociological fact that people of all classes, professions, ages, and states of life belong to our Association: men and women, clergy and laity, old and young, celibate and married people, university men, industrial and agricultural workers, clerks, members of the professions, people who work in official institutions, and so on. Have you considered the great power of spreading Christianity represented by such a broad and varied spectrum of people; especially if they are counted in tens of thousands and are animated with the same apostolic spirit to sanctify their profession or job, regardless of differences of social environment, to sanctify themselves in that work and to sanctify with that work?

To this personal apostolic work should be added the growth of our corporate works of apostolate: student residences, conference centers, the University of Navarre, training centers for skilled and unskilled workers, technical institutes, schools, secretarial colleges, home management schools, and so forth. These centers are undoubtedly sources which project the Christian view of life. Run by laymen, directed as *professional activities by lay citizens who are the same as their colleagues at work*, and open to people of all classes and conditions, these centers have made many sectors of society appreciate the need of offering a Christian solution to the problems which arise in the exercise of their profession or job.

All of this gives Opus Dei prominence and significance in society—not the fact that some of its members occupy positions of human influence. This does not interest us in the least, and is left therefore to the free decision and responsibility of each member. What interests us is that all the members—and the goodness of God is such that there are many—carry out tasks of which even the most humble are divinely influential.

This is quite logical. Who would say that the influence of the Church in the United States began on the day that a Catholic, John Kennedy, was elected President?

You have occasionally referred to Opus Dei as "organized unorganization." What exactly do you mean by this?

19   I mean that in our apostolate we give primary and fundamental importance to the spontaneity of the individual, to free and responsible initiative guided by the action of the Spirit,

and not to organizational structures, commands, and tactics imposed from above, from the seat of government.

There is obviously a minimum of organization, with a central government, which always acts collegiately and has its seat in Rome, and regional governments which are also collegiate, each headed by a Counselor.[2] But all the activity of these organisms is directed fundamentally to one task: to provide the members with the spiritual assistance necessary for their life of piety, and an adequate spiritual, doctrinal, religious, and human formation. And then, *off you go!* That is to say, Christians, sanctify all the paths of men, for all bear the imprint of the footsteps of God.

Having reached this point, the Association as such has done its job, the job precisely for which the members of Opus Dei have come together. The Association has nothing else to do. It neither can nor should it give any further indications. Here begins the free and responsible personal action of each member. Each one does his apostolate spontaneously, working with complete personal freedom. Autonomously forming his own conscience before the concrete decisions he has to take, he endeavors to seek Christian perfection and to give Christian witness in his own environment, sanctifying his own work, whether it be professional, intellectual, or manual. Naturally, as each one autonomously makes decisions in his secular life, in the temporal realities in which he moves, there will often be different options, criteria, and ways of acting. We have, in a word, that blessed *unorganization*, that just and necessary pluralism which is an essential characteristic of good spirit in Opus Dei, and which has always seemed to me the only just and orderly way to conceive the apostolate of the laity.

I will add that this *organized unorganization* appears even in the corporate works of apostolate which Opus Dei runs as an association, with the desire of contributing to resolve in a Christian way the problems which affect the community of each country. These activities and initiatives of the Association are always of a directly apostolic nature. They are educational or social welfare activities. But it is precisely our spirit to see that these initiatives should not come from above. And since the circumstances, needs, and possibilities of each nation or social group are unique, the central government of the Work leaves to the regional governments practically total autonomy. It is their responsibility to decide, foster, and organize the concrete apostolic activities which they consider most appropriate—a university center, a residence for students, a welfare center, or an agricultural college for farm workers. The logical result is that we have a multicolored and varied mosaic of activities, a mosaic which is *organizedly unorganized.*

In that case, how does Opus Dei fit into the pastoral action of the whole Church and into ecumenism?

20   I feel that I should first make something clear. Opus Dei is not, nor can it in any way be considered a reality tied to the evolutionary process of the "state of perfection" in the Church. It is not a modern or *up to date* form of that state. In fact, neither the theological concept of the *status perfectionis*, which Saint Thomas, Suarez, and other authors have decisively formulated in doctrine, nor the various juridical forms which have been given or may be given to this theological concept, have anything to do with the spirituality or the apostolic goal which God has wanted for our Association. I would simply point out, because a complete doctrinal exposition would take a long time, that Opus Dei is not interested in vows, or promises or any form of consecration for its members, apart from the consecration which all have already received through Baptism. Our Association in no way wants

its members to change their state in life or to stop being simple faithful exactly the same as anyone else, in order to acquire a *status perfectionis*. On the contrary, what it wants and endeavors is that each should do apostolate and should sanctify himself within his own state, in the place and condition which he has in the Church and in society. We take no one out of his place, nor do we separate anyone from his work or from his aims and noble commitments in the world.

Hence, the social reality, the spirituality, and the action of Opus Dei fit into a quite different vein in the life of the Church. They are in the theological and vital process which is bringing the laity to assume its responsibilities in the Church fully, and to participate in its own way in the mission of Christ and his Church. This has always been, during the nearly forty years of the Work's existence, the constant, calm but forceful concern through which God has desired to channel, in my soul and in the souls of my sons, the desire of serving him.

What contribution has Opus Dei made to this process? This is perhaps not the most suitable historical moment to attempt a general evaluation of this type. These questions were treated extensively, and with what joy to my soul, in the Second Vatican Council, and quite a few of the concepts and situations which refer to the life and mission of the laity have been sufficiently confirmed and illuminated by the Magisterium. Nevertheless, there remain a considerable number of questions which, for the vast majority, are still real *frontier problems* of theology. Most of these debated problems seem to us to be already divinely resolved, in the spirit which God has given to Opus Dei and which we endeavor to live faithfully, despite our personal imperfections. But we do not pretend to present these solutions as the only possible ones.

At the same time there are other aspects of this process of ecclesiological development which represent quite significant   21

doctrinal enrichments. God undoubtedly has desired that
Opus Dei, along with other no less worthy apostolic ventures
and associations, should contribute in no small part to them,
with its spirit and its life. However, these are doctrinal enrichments which may be long in becoming incorporated into the
life of the whole People of God. You yourself have touched
upon some of these aspects in your earlier questions: the
development of an authentic lay spirituality; the understanding of the layman's proper and specific role in the Church, a
role which is neither ecclesiastical nor official; the clarifi-
cation of the rights and duties which the layman has by virtue
of being a layman; the relations between hierarchy and laity;
the equality and dignity of the complementary, not contrary,
tasks which men and women have in the Church; the need to
achieve an orderly public opinion in the People of God, and
so forth.

All this obviously constitutes a very mobile reality, which
is often paradoxical. Something which when said forty years
ago scandalized most if not all who heard it, now sounds
strange to hardly anyone. But, on the other hand, there are
still very few who understand it fully and who live it properly.

I can explain this better with an example. In 1932, commenting for my sons and daughters in Opus Dei on some of
the aspects and consequences of the special dignity and responsibility which Baptism confers upon people, I wrote for
them in a document, "The prejudice that ordinary members
of the faithful must limit themselves to helping the clergy in
ecclesiastical apostolates has to be rejected. There is no reason why the secular apostolate should always be a mere participation in the apostolate of the hierarchy. Secular people
too have a duty to do apostolate. Not because they receive a
canonical mission, but because they are part of the Church.
Their mission . . . is fulfilled in their profession, their job,
their family, and among their colleagues and friends."

Today, after the solemn teachings of Vatican II, it is un-likely that anyone in the Church would question the ortho-doxy of this teaching. But how many people have really abandoned the narrow conception of the apostolate of the laity as a pastoral work *organized from the top down?* How many people have got beyond the previous "monolithic" con-ception of the lay apostolate and understand that it can and indeed should exist without the necessity of rigid centralized structures, canonical missions, and hierarchical mandates? How many people who consider the laity as the *longa manus Ecclesiae*, do not at the same time confuse in their minds the concept of Church-People of God with the more limited concept of hierarchy? How many laymen understand that unless they act in tactful communion with the hierarchy they have no right to claim their legitimate sphere of apostolic autonomy?

Similar lines of thought could be formulated with regard to other problems, because there is in fact a great deal which remains to be done, as much in the way of doctrinal exposi-tion, as by education of consciences and reform of ecclesias-tical legislation. I often ask our Lord—prayer has always been my great weapon—that the Holy Spirit will help his People, and especially the hierarchy, in accomplishing these tasks. And I also ask him to continue using Opus Dei so that we may be able to contribute and help, in whatever way we can, in this difficult but wonderful process of development and growth in the Church.

You also wanted to know *how Opus Dei fits into ecu-menism.* Last year I told a French journalist—and I know that the anecdote has been retold, even in publications of our separated brethren—what I once told the Holy Father John XXIII, moved by the affable and fatherly kindness of his man-ner: "Holy Father, in our Work all men, Catholics or not, have always found a welcome. I have not learned ecumenism from your Holiness." He laughed, for he knew that way back in 1950 the Holy See had authorized Opus Dei to receive in the Association as Cooperators people who are not Catholics or even Christians.

In fact, there are many separated brethren who feel attracted by the spirit of Opus Dei and who cooperate in our apostolates, and they include ministers and even bishops of their respective confessions. As contacts increase, we receive more and more proofs of affection and cordial understanding. And it is because the members of Opus Dei center their spirituality simply on trying to live responsibly the commitments and demands of Christian baptism. A desire to seek Christian perfection and to do apostolate, endeavoring to sanctify their own professional work; the fact of living immersed in secular reality and respecting its proper autonomy, but dealing with it with the spirit and love of contemplative souls; the primacy which we give in the organization of our apostolate to the individual, to the action of the Spirit upon souls, to the dignity and freedom which derive from the divine filiation of Christians; the defense of the legitimate freedom of initiative, within a necessary respect for the common good, against the monolithic and institutionalistic conception of the apostolate of the laity: these and other aspects of our way of being and acting are so many points of easy contact with our separated brethren. Here they find, put into living practice, a good many of the doctrinal presuppositions in which they, and we Catholics, have placed so many well-founded ecumenical expectations.

Turning to another topic, we would like to know your opinion regarding the present situation of the Church. How would you describe it? What role do you think can be played in these times by the tendencies which in general terms have been called "progressive" and "integrist"?

As I see it, the present doctrinal position of the Church could   23
be expressed as "positive" and at the same time "delicate," as
in all crises of growth. Positive, undoubtedly, because the
doctrinal wealth of the Second Vatican Council has set the
entire Church, the entire priestly People of God, on a new
supremely hopeful track of renewed fidelity to the divine
plan of salvation which has been entrusted to it. But delicate
as well, because the theological conclusions which have
been reached are not, let us say, of an abstract or theoretical
nature. They are part of a supremely *living* theology, which
has immediate and direct applications in the pastoral, ascetic,
and disciplinary fields and which touches very deeply the
internal and external life of the Church: liturgy, organizational
structures of the hierarchy, apostolic forms, Magisterium, dialogue with the world, ecumenism. And therefore at the same
time this theology touches very deeply the Christian life and
the very conscience of the faithful.

Both aspects affect us deeply: both Christian optimism,
the joyful certainty that the Holy Spirit will draw fruit from
the doctrine with which he has enriched the Spouse of
Christ; and also prudence on the part of those who study and
govern because, now especially, immense harm could result
from a lack of serenity and consideration in the study of these
problems.

As regards the tendencies which you call *integrist* and
progressive, I find it difficult to give an opinion on the role
which they can play at the present moment, because I have
always rejected the suitability and even the possibility of making classifications or simplifications of this sort. This division
is at times taken to great extremes and perpetuated as if
theologians (and the faithful in general) were destined always
to be circling these opposite poles. As far as I can see, it
seems to derive ultimately from the belief that progress in the
doctrine and in the life of the People of God is the result of a

perpetual dialectical tension. I, on the other hand, prefer to believe wholeheartedly in the action of the Holy Spirit, who breathes where he will and upon whom he will.

Why Opus Dei?

Interview with Peter Forbarth (*Time* magazine)
—April 15, 1967

Would you explain the central mission and objectives of Opus Dei? On what precedent did you base your ideas for the Association? Or is Opus Dei something unique, totally new within the Church and Christianity? Can it be compared with religious orders and secular institutes, or with Catholic organizations like the Holy Name Society, the Knights of Columbus, or the Christopher Movement?

Opus Dei aims to encourage people of every sector of society   24
to desire holiness in the midst of the world. In other words, Opus Dei proposes to help ordinary citizens like yourself to lead a fully Christian life, without modifying their normal way of life, their daily work, their aspirations and ambitions.

As I wrote years ago, you could say that Opus Dei is as old and as new as the gospel. It intends to remind Christians of the wonderful words of Genesis: God created man to work. We try to imitate the example of Christ, who spent almost all his life on earth working as a carpenter in a small town. Work is one of the highest human values and the way in which men contribute to the progress of society. But even more, it is a way to holiness.

With what other organizations can Opus Dei be compared? That question is not easy to answer. When one compares organizations which have spiritual aims, there is always a risk of considering external features or juridical status to the detriment of what is more important, the spirit that animates them and is the *raison d'etre* of all their activities.

I shall merely say that with respect to the organizations you mentioned, Opus Dei is very far removed from religious orders and secular institutes and closer to institutions like the Holy Name Society. Opus Dei is an international lay organization to which a certain number of secular priests belong, although they are a small minority. Its members are people who live in the world and hold normal jobs. They do not join Opus Dei to give up their job. On the contrary, what they look for in the Work is the spiritual help they need to sanctify their ordinary work. Thus their work becomes a means to sanctify themselves and help others to do the same thing. They do not change their status. They continue being single, married, widowed, or priests. What they try to do is serve God and their fellow men in their own state in life. Opus Dei is not interested in vows or promises. It asks its members to make an effort to practice human and Christian virtues, as children of God, despite the limitations and errors that are inevitable in human life.

If you want a point of comparison, the easiest way to understand Opus Dei is to consider the life of the early Christians. They lived their Christian vocation seriously, seeking earnestly the holiness to which they had been called by their Baptism. Externally they did nothing to distinguish themselves from their fellow citizens. The members of Opus Dei are ordinary people. They work like everyone else and live in the midst of the world just as they did before they joined. There is nothing false or artificial about their behavior. They live like any other Christian citizen who wants to respond fully to the demands of his faith, because that is what they are.

I would like to insist on the question of secular institutes. I have read a study by a well-known canonist, Dr Julián Herranz,[1] which affirms that some secular institutes are

secret and others are practically indistinguishable from
religious orders since their members wear habits and give
up their professional work to dedicate their lives to the
same aims as religious, up to the point of having no
objection to being considered religious. What do you
think about this?

The study on secular institutes you mentioned has been   25
widely read and discussed by specialists in the field. Dr.
Herranz undoubtedly brings to bear a great deal of evidence
to support the thesis [2] he personally defends, but I prefer not
to comment on the conclusions he draws.

I can only say that that way of acting has nothing whatsoever to do with Opus Dei. The Work is not secret and neither
its activities nor the life of its members make it in any way
comparable to religious orders. Opus Dei members, as I just
said, are workaday citizens, exactly the same as other citizens,
who freely practice any honest [3] profession or occupation.

Would you describe how Opus Dei has developed and
evolved, both in its character and objectives, since its
founding, a period that has witnessed enormous changes
within the Church itself?

From its very beginning, Opus Dei's only aim has been what   26
I have just described: to contribute to there being in the
midst of the world men and women of every race and social
condition who try to love and serve God and their fellow men
in and through their everyday work. Since the foundation of
the Work in 1928, my teaching has been that sanctity is not
reserved for a privileged few. All the ways of the earth,
every state in life, every profession, every honest task can be
divine.

This message has numerous implications which the life of

the Work has helped me to grasp with ever greater depth and clarity. The Work was born small and has grown up normally, little by little, like a living organism, like everything that develops in history. But its objectives have not changed. Nor will they change, no matter how greatly society may be transformed. Opus Dei's message is that under all circumstances any honest work can be sanctified.

People from all walks of life belong to Opus Dei: doctors, lawyers, engineers, and artists, as well as bricklayers, miners, and farm laborers. All professions are represented, from film directors and jet pilots to high-fashion hairdressers. It is perfectly natural for Opus Dei members to be up to date with modern developments and to understand the world. Together with their fellow citizens, who are their equals, they are part of the contemporary world and make it modern.

In the light of Opus Dei's spirit, it was clearly a great joy for us to see the Council solemnly declare that the Church does not reject the world it lives in, with its progress and development, but understands and loves it. Furthermore, the members of the Work are keenly aware of the fact that they are at one and the same time part of the Church and of society, and they assume individually their personal responsibility as Christians and as citizens. This is a characteristic feature of Opus Dei's spirituality which its members have endeavored to live since its foundation nearly forty years ago.

Could you describe the differences in the way Opus Dei as an association fulfills its mission and Opus Dei members as individuals fulfill theirs: for example, by what criteria is a project deemed best undertaken by the Association, such as a school or conference center, or by individuals, such as a publishing or commercial venture?

Opus Dei's main activity consists in offering its members, and 27 other people, the spiritual means they need to live as good Christians in the midst of the world. It helps them to learn Christ's doctrine and the Church's teachings. Its spirit moves them to work well for the love of God and as a service to other men. In a word, it helps them to behave like genuine Christians: being loyal friends, respecting the legitimate freedom of others, and trying to make our world more just.

Each member earns his living and serves society in the job he held before joining the Work and would hold if he did not belong to Opus Dei. There are miners, teachers, housewives, shopkeepers, university professors, secretaries, farmers, and on and on. A member of Opus Dei can carry out any noble human activity; no honest work is excluded. For instance, a publisher or a businessman who joins the Work continues to hold the position he held before. And if he looks for a new job, or decides with other businessmen to form a company of one sort or another, he decides freely, accepting personally the results of his work and answering personally for its success or failure.

All the activity of Opus Dei's directors is based on a great respect for the members' professional freedom. This point is of capital importance. The Work's very existence depends on it, so no exceptions are admitted. A member's job is in no way related to his membership. Consequently, neither the Work nor any of the other members has anything to do with his professional activities. Joining the Work only implies an obligation to make an honest effort to seek holiness in and through one's job and to be more fully aware of the service to humanity that every Christian life should be.

As I was saying, Opus Dei's principal mission is to give a Christian training to its members and to others who desire it. However, moved by a desire to contribute to the solution of each society's problems, which are so closely related to the

Christian ideal, it also has some other *corporate* activities. Our criterion in this field is that Opus Dei, whose aims are exclusively spiritual, can only carry out corporatively activities which clearly constitute an immediate Christian service, an apostolate. It would be ridiculous to think that Opus Dei as such could mine coal or run any type of commercial venture. Its corporate works are all directly apostolic activities: training centers for farm workers, medical dispensaries in developing countries or areas, schools for girls from underprivileged families. In other words, educational or welfare activities like those carried on throughout the world by organizations of every religious creed.

In these activities we count in the first place on the work of Opus Dei members who occasionally work full time in them. And also on the generous aid of many other people, Christian and non-Christian alike. Some of them help us for spiritual reasons. Others do not share our apostolic motives, but they see that these activities benefit society and are open to everyone, without any kind of racial, religious, or ideological[4] discrimination.

Members of Opus Dei are present in all social strata and some of them hold positions as directors of important companies and groups. Could it be affirmed that Opus Dei tries to coordinate their activities following a particular political or economic line?

28   No. Opus Dei has nothing whatever to do with politics. It is absolutely foreign to any political, economic, ideological, or cultural tendency or group. Let me repeat that its aims are exclusively spiritual and apostolic. The only thing it demands of its members is that they lead a Christian life, trying to live up to the ideal of the gospel. Therefore it never becomes involved in any temporal affair.

If someone does not understand this, it may well be because he does not understand personal freedom, or because he is incapable of distinguishing between the purely spiritual ends for which the members of the Work are associated and the vast field of human activities (economics, politics, culture, art, philosophy, for example) in which they enjoy complete freedom and act on their own responsibility.

From the moment in which they first approach the Work, all its members are fully aware of their individual freedom. If one of them ever tried to exert pressure on the others to make them accept his political opinions, or to use them for human interests, they would rebel and expel him without a second thought.

Respect for its members' liberty is an essential condition of Opus Dei's very existence. Without it, no one would come to the Work. Even more. The Work has never intervened in politics and, with God's help, it never will; but if it were to, I would be its number one enemy.

Opus Dei places great emphasis on the individual and the freedom of the individual to express his honestly held convictions. But returning to my previous question from another point of view, to what degree do you feel that Opus Dei is morally obliged as an association to express opinions on crucial secular and spiritual issues either publicly or privately? Are there situations in which Opus Dei will bring its own and its membership's influence to bear in defense of principles it holds sacred, for example, in support of religious freedom legislation in Spain recently?

In Opus Dei, we always strive to be in full agreement with   29
Christ's Church in our opinions and sentiments; *sentire cum Ecclesia.* Our doctrine is no more and no less than what the

Church teaches all the faithful. The only thing which is proper to Opus Dei is its characteristic spirit, that is to say, its concrete way of living the gospel, sanctifying oneself in the world and carrying out an apostolate through one's profession.

As an immediate consequence, a member of Opus Dei enjoys the same freedom as any other Catholic to form his own opinions and to act accordingly. Therefore, Opus Dei as such neither should nor can express—nor even have—an opinion of its own. If on a given question the Church has defined a doctrine, the members of Opus Dei adhere to it. If, on the other hand, the official teaching of the Church—the Pope and the bishops—has said nothing on a question, each member of Opus Dei holds and defends the opinion he sees fit, and acts in consequence.

In other words, the principle which governs the activity of Opus Dei's directors in this field is respect for freedom of opinion in temporal matters. It is not a form of abstentionism. It is, rather, a question of making each individual aware of his own responsibilities and of inviting him to accept them according to the dictates of his conscience, acting with full freedom. It would therefore be incongruous to mention Opus Dei in a context of parties, political groups, and tendencies, or of human enterprises and undertakings. More than incongruous, it would be unjust and incipient libel, for it could easily lead someone to deduce falsely that Opus Dei members share the same ideology, outlook, or temporal interest.

Undoubtedly they are Catholics, and Catholics who strive to be consistent with their faith, so one can classify them as such if he likes. But he should bear in mind that being Catholic does not imply belonging to a closed cultural or ideological group, and much less to a particular political party. From the very beginning of the Work, not only since the Council, we have striven to live broad-minded Catholicism, a Catholicism that defends the legitimate liberty of every individual's conscience and leads us to treat all men (Catholics or not) as brothers and to collaborate with them, sharing their noble ideals.

We might take as an example the racial problems in the United States. With respect to this problem, an American Opus Dei member will be orientated by the clear Christian principle of the equality of all men and the injustice of any type of discrimination. Furthermore, he will be guided by the concrete indications of the American bishops on the question. He will, therefore, defend the legitimate rights of all citizens and oppose any discriminatory situation or project. Finally, he will bear in mind that a Christian cannot be satisfied with merely respecting the rights of others. He has to see in every man a brother to whom he owes sincere love and disinterested service.

These ideas occupy a more important place in the formation Opus Dei gives its members in the United States than in other countries where the problem is less grave or nonexistent. But Opus Dei can never dictate, or even suggest, a concrete solution for the problem. Each member has to decide for himself whether to back or oppose a particular bill, to join one civil rights movement or another (or not to join any at all), to participate or not in a demonstration. And in fact in all parts of the world it is easy to observe the pluralism of Opus Dei members and see that they do not act as a group.

These same criteria explain the fact that so many Spanish members of Opus Dei are favorable to the recently proposed religious liberty bill in Spain. Their decision is a personal one, as is that of those who oppose this particular bill. But all of them have been taught by the spirit of the Work to love freedom and to understand people of every creed. Opus Dei is the first Catholic organization that (since 1950) has the Holy See's permission to admit as cooperators people who are non-Catholics and non-Christians, without discrimination of any kind, with love for all.

You are, of course, aware of the somewhat controversial reputation enjoyed by Opus Dei in certain sections of public opinion. Could you give your opinion on why this is so, and especially how does one answer the charge of "conspiratorial secrecy" and "secret conspiracy" often levelled against Opus Dei?

30   I detest everything that could sound like self-praise, but since you have brought up the subject I cannot fail to say that in my opinion Opus Dei is one of the best-loved Catholic organizations in the world. Millions of people, and among them many non-Catholics and non-Christians, are good friends of the Work and help us in our apostolic activities.

Opus Dei is a spiritual and apostolic organization. If one forgets this fundamental fact, or refuses to believe in the good faith of the members of the Work who affirm it, it is impossible to understand what we do. And this very lack of understanding can lead people to invent complicated stories and secrets which have never existed.

You speak of charges of secrecy. All that is now ancient history. I could explain, point by point, the origin of those calumnious charges. A powerful organization I prefer not to name but which we esteem and have always esteemed spent its energies over many years falsifying what it did not understand. They insisted on considering us monks or friars and asked, "Why don't they all think the same way? Why don't they wear a religious habit or at least a badge?" And they reached the completely illogical conclusion that we were some sort of secret society.

Now all that belongs to the past. Any reasonably well-informed person knows that there is nothing secret about

Opus Dei. We do not wear a habit or badge because we are ordinary Christians, not religious. We do not all think the same way because we admit the greatest possible pluralism in all temporal matters and in debatable theological questions. A more accurate knowledge of the facts and the disappearance of unfounded fears have put an end to a situation in which false accusations were lamentably frequent.

It is not surprising, however, that every now and then someone tries to stir up old myths. The fact that we strive to work for God, defending the personal freedom of all men, means that we will always meet with the opposition of all the sectarian enemies of freedom. And they will be all the more aggressive if they are religious fanatics or people who cannot stand the idea of religion.

Fortunately, nonetheless, the majority of publications are not content with repeating old falsehoods and realize that impartiality does not consist in publishing something halfway between reality and what detractors say, but rather in reflecting objective truth. I personally feel the truth can also be *news*, especially when it is a question of giving information about the activities of the thousands of men and women who belong to Opus Dei or who cooperate with it, striving to carry out a task in benefit of mankind despite their personal errors—I commit them and I am not surprised that others do so. Exploding a false myth is always worthwhile. To my mind a journalist has a grave moral obligation to look for accurate information and to keep up to date, even though it may imply changing previous judgments. Is it really so difficult to admit that something is noble, honest, and good, without mixing in absurd, old-fashioned, and discredited falsehoods?

It is easy to get to know Opus Dei. It works in broad daylight in all countries, with the full juridical recognition of the civil and ecclesiastical authorities. The names of its directors and of its apostolic undertakings are well known.

Anyone who wants information can obtain it without difficulty, contacting its directors or going to one of its centers. You yourself can testify that Opus Dei's directors and the personnel in charge of taking care of journalists never fail to offer all the necessary facilities, answering questions and giving out printed information.

Neither I nor any of the members of Opus Dei expect everyone to understand us or to share our spiritual ideals. I respect everyone's liberty, and I want each person to follow his own path in life. But obviously we too have an elementary right to be respected.

How do you explain the enormous success of Opus Dei, and by what criteria do you measure this success?

31   When an undertaking is supernatural, its "success" or "failure" in the ordinary sense of the word is relatively unimportant. As Saint Paul said to the Christians at Corinth, what matters in the spiritual life is not what others think of us, or even our own opinion of ourselves, but God's opinion.

Undoubtedly the Work has spread all over the world. Men and women of close to seventy nationalities now belong to it. To tell the truth, it is something that surprises me. I cannot provide any human explanation for it. The only explanation is the will of God, for "the Spirit breathes where he will" and he makes use of whomever he sees fit to sanctify men. For me it is an occasion for thanksgiving, for humility, and for asking God for the grace to serve him always.

You also asked by what criteria I measure and judge. The answer is very simple: sanctity, fruits of sanctity.

Opus Dei's most important apostolate is the testimony of the life and conversation of each individual member in his daily contacts with his friends and fellow workers. Who can measure the supernatural effectiveness of this quiet and humble apostolate? It is impossible to evaluate the help we receive from a loyal and sincere friend or the influence of a good mother over her family.

But perhaps your question refers to the corporate apostolates carried out by Opus Dei, supposing that their results can be measured from a human or technical viewpoint: whether a technical training center for workers contributes to the social advancement of its pupils, whether a university offers its students an adequate cultural and professional formation. If that was your intention, I would say that their results can be explained in part by the fact that they are undertakings carried out by carefully trained professionals who are practicing their own profession. This implies, among other things, that these activities are planned in every case in the light of the particular necessities of the society in which they are to be carried out, and adapted to real needs, not according to preconceived schemes.

But let me repeat that Opus Dei is not primarily interested in human effectiveness. The real success or failure of our activities depends on whether, in addition to being humanly well-run, they help those who carry them out and those who make use of their services to love God, to feel their brotherhood with their fellow men, and to manifest those sentiments in a disinterested service of humanity.

Would you describe how and why you founded Opus Dei and the events that you consider the major milestones in its development.

Why? The only explanation for things that are born of God's will is that he has wanted to use them as an expression of his desire to save all men. From the first moment, the Work was universal, catholic. It was born not to solve the concrete problems facing Europe in the '20s, but to tell men and   32 women of every country and of every condition, race, language, milieu, and state in life (single, married, widowed, or priests) that they can love and serve God without giving up their ordinary work, their family life, and their normal social relations.

How was it founded? Without any human means. I was a twenty-six-year-old priest with nothing but God's grace and good humor. The Work was born very small. It was only a young priest's desire to do what God asked of him.

You asked me for milestones. For me every time the Work helps a soul draw closer to God and therefore become more of a brother of his fellow men it is an important milestone in the history of Opus Dei.

I could also mention some crucial dates. Although they may not be the most important, I will give you a few approximate ones by memory. Early in 1935 we were ready to begin working in France, as a matter of fact in Paris. But then the Spanish Civil War broke out and afterward the Second World War, and we had to put off the expansion of the Work. But since expansion was necessary, the delay was minimal. In 1940 our work in Portugal began. After a few preliminary trips in previous years, practically coinciding with the end of the hostilities it began in England, Italy, France, the United States, and Mexico. Afterward the rhythm of growth and expansion became more rapid. From 1949 and 1950 on: in Germany, Ireland, Holland, Switzerland, Argentina, Canada, Venezuela, and the other European and South American countries. Simultaneously we began in other continents: in North Africa, Japan, Kenya and the other East African countries, Australia, Philippines, Nigeria.

I also like to recall the numerous occasions on which the Popes have shown more tangibly their affection for our Work. I have resided in Rome since 1946, so I have been fortunate enough to know personally Pius XII, John XXIII, and Paul VI.

All three of them have always shown truly paternal affection for us.

Would you agree with the statement which is occasionally made that special conditions in Spain during the last thirty years have contributed to Opus Dei's growth there?

In very few places have we had fewer facilities than in Spain.   33
I don't like to say so, because I naturally love my country deeply, but it is in Spain that we have had the greatest difficulties in making the Work take root. No sooner had it been born, than it met with the opposition of all the enemies of personal freedom and of people who were so attached to traditional ideas that they could not understand the life of Opus Dei members, ordinary Christians who strive to live their Christian vocation fully without leaving the world.

The situation in Spain with respect to our corporate apostolates has not been particularly favorable either. The governments of countries where Catholics are a minority have helped the educational and welfare activities founded by Opus Dei members far more generously than the Spanish government. The aid those governments grant Opus Dei's corporate activities, like that they usually give other similar centers, is not a privilege, but a just recognition of their social function and of the money they save the taxpayers.

In the course of its international expansion, Opus Dei's spirit has been very well received in all countries. Our difficulties have in large part been the result of falsehoods originating in Spain. They were invented by members of certain well-defined sectors of Spanish society; in the first place, by the international organization I mentioned before, but fortunately that seems to belong to the past and I don't hold a grudge against anyone. Another sector is composed of people characterized by partisanship, when not by narrow-mindedness or a totalitarian mentality, who do not understand pluralism and who use their reputation as Catholics for political purposes. I don't know how to explain why, but some of them seem to take special pleasure in attacking Opus Dei, perhaps for false human reasons. Since they can finance them amply with the Spanish taxpayer's money, their attacks are reproduced in certain sectors of the press.

I am perfectly aware that you would like me to name concrete persons and institutions, but I hope you will understand why I do not do so. Neither my mission nor Opus Dei's is political; my business is to pray. I don't want to say anything that could possibly be interpreted as an intervention in politics. In fact, I would prefer not to have to even mention the subject. I have held my peace for almost forty years, and if I say anything now it is only because I have an obligation to denounce as absolutely false the distorted picture that has been given of our exclusively spiritual work. And for that very reason, although I have kept silent until now, I intend to speak out in the future, even more clearly if necessary.

Getting back to the main subject of your question, if many people of all social classes, in Spain and throughout the world, have decided to follow Christ with the Work's help, living its spirit, the explanation is not to be found in the environment nor in other external factors. Proof of it lies in the fact that the very people who so lightly affirm the contrary have seen their own groups shrink; and the external factors are the same for everyone. Perhaps a partial explanation, from the human point of view, is that they form closed groups, while we don't deprive anyone of his personal freedom.

If in Spain (as in several other countries) Opus Dei is quite well developed, it may well be because our spiritual work began there forty years ago, and, as I mentioned before, the Spanish Civil War and the Second World War made it necessary to postpone our extension to other countries. Nevertheless, I want to add that for a number of years we Spaniards have been a minority in the Work.

I wouldn't like you to think that I do not love my country or that I am not extremely pleased with the activity the Work carries out there. But it is a shame that falsehoods are occasionally disseminated about Opus Dei and Spain.

The Apostolate of Opus Dei
on Five Continents

Interview with Jacques Guillemé-Brûlon (*Le Figaro*)
—published May 16, 1966

People have sometimes said that Opus Dei was organized internally along the lines of secret societies. What is to be thought of such a statement? Could you give us, with this in mind, your own idea of the message you wanted to address to the men of our time when you founded the Work in 1928?

34 Ever since 1928 my preaching has been that sanctity is not reserved for the privileged few and that all the ways of the earth can be divine. The reason is that the spirituality of Opus Dei is based on the sanctification of ordinary work. The prejudice must be rejected that the ordinary faithful can do no more than limit themselves to helping the clergy in ecclesiastical apostolates. It should be remembered that to attain this supernatural end men need to be and to feel personally free with the freedom Christ won for us.

To proclaim and to teach how to practice this doctrine I have never needed anything secret. The members of the Work detest secrecy because they are ordinary faithful, the same as anyone else. They do not change their status when they join Opus Dei. It would be repulsive for them to carry a sign on their backs that said, "Let it be known that I am dedicated to the service of God." That would be neither lay nor secular. But those who associate with members of Opus Dei and are acquainted with them realize that they belong to the Work, for, even if they do not publicize their membership, neither do they hide it.

Could you give a brief picture of the worldwide structure of Opus Dei and of its relations with the General Council in Rome over which you preside?

The General Council, which is independent for each section—the men's and the women's—resides in Rome.[1] A corresponding organization exists in each country, presided over by the Counselor of Opus Dei in that nation.[2]

35

But do not imagine a powerful organization, spread out like a vast network to the farthest corners of the world. Rather, imagine an *unorganized organization* in which the principal work of the Directors is to see that all the members receive the genuine spirit of the Gospels (a spirit of charity, of harmony, of understanding, all of which are absolutely foreign to extremism) by means of a solid and appropriate theological and apostolic training. Beyond this each member acts with complete personal freedom. He forms his conscience autonomously. And he tries to seek Christian perfection and to Christianize his environment, by sanctifying his own work, whether it be intellectual or manual, in all the circumstances of his life and in his own home.

Furthermore, direction in the Work is always collegial. We detest tyranny, especially in the exclusively spiritual government of Opus Dei. We love pluralism. The contrary would only lead to ineffectiveness, to neither getting things done nor letting others do them, to never improving.

Point 484 in your spiritual code, The Way, *specifies: "Your duty is to be an instrument." What meaning should be given to this statement in the context of the preceding questions?*

36   *The Way* a code? Not at all. I wrote a good part of that book in 1934, summarizing my priestly experience for the benefit of all the souls with whom I was in contact, whether they were in Opus Dei or not. I never suspected that thirty years later it would be spread so widely—millions of copies, in so many languages. It is not a book solely for members of Opus Dei. It is for everyone, whether Christian or non-Christian. Among those who have translated it on their own initiative are Orthodox, Protestants, and non-Christians. *The Way* must be read with at least some supernatural spirit, interior life, and apostolic feeling. It is not a code for the man of action. The book's aim is to help men to become God's friends, to love him, and to serve all men. In other words, to be an instrument—which gets back to your question—as Paul the Apostle wanted to be, an instrument of Christ, a free and responsible instrument. Anyone who tries to see a temporal goal in the pages of *The Way* is mistaken. Do not forget that it has been common for spiritual authors of every age to see souls as instruments in the hands of God.

Does Spain occupy a preferred position in the Work? Can it be considered the starting point of a more ambitious program, or is it just another area of activity among so many others?

37   Of the sixty-five countries from which Opus Dei members come, Spain is merely one among others, and we Spaniards are in the minority. Geographically, Opus Dei was born in Spain. But from the beginning its aim has been universal. And I myself have lived in Rome for twenty years.

Hasn't the fact that some members of the Work are active in the public life of Spain politicized Opus Dei in that country in some way? Don't they compromise the Work, and even the Church?

No, not in Spain, or in any other place. I insist that each of the   38
members of Opus Dei carries on his work with full freedom
and with personal responsibility. They compromise neither
the Church nor the Work, for they are supported neither by
the Church nor by the Work in their personal activities.
People who have a military concept of apostolate and
spiritual life will always tend to see the free and personal
work of Christians as a collective activity. But I assure you, as
I have said again and again since 1928, that variety in thought
and action in what is temporal and in what is a matter of
theological opinion poses no problem for the Work. On the
contrary, the diversity which exists and always will exist
among the members of Opus Dei is a sign of good spirit, of
an honest life, of respect for the legitimate opinion of each
individual.

*Do you not believe that in Spain, by reason of the particu-
larism inherent in the Iberian people, a group within the
Work could be tempted to use its power to satisfy particular interests?*

You have formulated a hypothesis which I dare to guarantee   39
will never occur in the Work. Not only because we associate
exclusively for supernatural ends, but also because if a member of Opus Dei should attempt to impose, directly or indi-
rectly, a temporal criterion on the other members, or if he
should try to make use of them for human ends, he would be
expelled at once. For the other members would rebel, and
their rebellion would be legitimate and holy.

*In Spain Opus Dei prides itself on including people in
all walks of life. Is this valid for the rest of the world, or
must it be admitted that in other countries the members
of Opus Dei come from the upper classes such as the top*

levels of industry, the civil service, politics, and the professions?

40   In Spain and in the whole world, people of all social conditions belong to Opus Dei: men and women, old and young, workers, businessmen, clerks, farmers, members of the professions, and so forth. It is God who gives the vocation, and with God there is no distinction of persons.

But Opus Dei does not pride itself on anything. Apostolic undertakings grow, not by human effort, but by the breathing of the Holy Spirit. It is reasonable for an association with earthly aims to publish impressive statistics on the number, social standing, and qualities of its members. And, in fact, organizations in search of temporal prestige usually do so. But when the sanctification of souls is the aim, to act in such a way would encourage triumphalism, whereas Christ wants each individual Christian, personally, and the whole Christian body, collectively, to be humble.

How is the Work developing in France at the present time?

41   As I was telling you, the government of the Work in each country is autonomous. You can obtain the best information on the work of Opus Dei in France by asking the Directors of the Work in that country. But among the activities Opus Dei carries on corporately, for which Opus Dei as such is responsible, there are student residences like the Residence Internationale de Rouvray in Paris and the Residence Universitaire de l'Ile Verte in Grenoble; conference centers like the Centre de Rencontres Couvrelles in the Department of Aisne; and so forth.

But let me remind you that the corporate works are the least important thing. The main task of Opus Dei is the direct, personal witness which the members give in the practice of their own ordinary work. And for this, it is useless to count the members. But do not think about the ghost of secrecy. By no means. The birds that fill the skies are no secret, but no one thinks of counting them.

What is the present status of the Work in the rest of the world, especially in the English-speaking countries?

Opus Dei feels as much at home in England as in Kenya, in   42
Nigeria as in Japan, in the United States as in Austria, in Ireland as in Mexico or Argentina. In each place it is the same theological and pastoral phenomenon which takes root in the souls of the people of that country. It is not anchored in one particular culture nor in one specific historical period.

In the English-speaking world, thanks to God's help and the cooperation of very many people, Opus Dei has apostolic works of different types: Netherhall House in London, devoted to Afro-Asian students; Hudson Centre in Montreal, for the human and intellectual development of young women; Warrane College, for the students of Sydney. In the United States, where Opus Dei began to work in 1949, one could mention Midtown, a center for workers in the Near West Side of Chicago; Stonecrest Community Center in Washington, for the education of women who lack professional training; Trimount House, a university residence in Boston; and so forth.

One final remark: the Work's influence, so far as it exists in each case, will always be spiritual and of a religious, never a temporal, nature.

Various sources assume that a solid enmity sets most religious orders, and especially the Jesuits, in opposition to Opus Dei. Do these rumors have any foundation at all, or are they one of those myths which people build up when they are not well acquainted with a problem?

43   We are not religious. We bear no resemblance to religious nor is there any authority on earth which could require us to be religious. Yet in Opus Dei we venerate and love the religious state. I pray every day that all venerable religious will continue to offer the Church the fruits of their virtues, their apostolic works, and their holiness. The rumors you spoke of are just that—rumors. Opus Dei has always enjoyed the admiration and the sympathetic good will of religious of many orders and congregations, especially of cloistered monks and nuns, who pray for us, write us often, and make our work known in a thousand ways because they can appreciate the meaning of our life: contemplatives in the midst of the cares of the secular city.

The Secretary General of Opus Dei, Alvaro del Portillo, was a friend of the last General of the Jesuits. I am equally close to the present General, Father Arrupe, and have a high regard for him.

Misunderstandings, if they should occur, would show a lack of Christian spirit, for our faith calls for unity, not for rivalries or divisions.

What is the position of the Work as regards the Council's Declaration on Religious Freedom, and especially as regards its application in Spain, where the "Castiella Project" is still suspended? And what about the alleged "integrism" for which Opus Dei has occasionally been reproached?

44   Integrism? Opus Dei is neither on the right nor on the left nor in the center. As a priest I strive to be with Christ. Both of his arms—not just one—were outstretched on the cross. I freely take from every group whatever seems good to me and helps me to keep my heart and my two arms open to all mankind. And every member of Opus Dei is also utterly free, within the bounds of the Christian faith, to hold whatever opinion he likes.

As regards religious liberty, from its foundation Opus Dei has never practiced discrimination of any kind. It works and lives with everyone because it sees in each person a soul which must be respected and loved. These are not mere words. Our Work is the first Catholic organization which, with the authorization of the Holy See, admits non-Catholics, whether Christian or not, as Cooperators. I have always defended the freedom of individual consciences. I do not understand violence; I do not consider it a proper way either to persuade or to win over. Error is overcome by prayer, by God's grace, and by study; never by force; always with charity. From the first moment this is the spirit we have lived. You can understand, then, how the Council's teaching on this subject could only make me happy.

As to the specific project you refer to, it is not my problem to solve. It belongs to the Church's hierarchy in Spain and to the Catholics of that country. It is up to them to apply the Council's spirit to the case in question.

Some readers of The Way *are surprised by the statement in point 28: "Marriage is for the soldiers and not for the General Staff of Christ's army." Can that be taken as a disparaging appraisal of marriage, which would go against the Work's desire to be inserted in the living realities of the modern world?*

I advise you to read the previous point of *The Way*, which   45
states that marriage is a divine vocation—it was not at all frequent to hear that sort of affirmation around 1925.

The conclusions you spoke of could only spring from a failure to understand my words. With that metaphor I wanted to recall what the Church has always taught about the excellence and supernatural value of apostolic celibacy. At the same time I wanted to remind all Christians that they must consider themselves *milites Christi* (soldiers of Christ) in Saint Paul's words, members of the People of God who are engaged on earth in a divine warfare of understanding, holiness, and peace. All over the world there are many thousands of married couples who belong to Opus Dei or who live according to its spirit. And they are well aware that a soldier may be decorated for bravery in the same battle from which the general shamefully fled.

You established your residence in Rome in 1946. What is there about the Pontiffs you have dealt with that stands out in your memory?

46   For me, in the hierarchy of love, the Pope comes right after the most holy Trinity and our Mother the Virgin. I cannot forget that it was his Holiness Pius XII who approved Opus Dei at a time when some people considered our spirituality a *heresy*. Nor can I forget that the first words of kindness and affection I received in Rome in 1946 came from the then Monsignor Montini. The affable and paternal charm of John XXIII, every time I had occasion to visit him, remains engraved in my memory. Once I told him: "In our Work all men, Catholics or not, have always been lovingly received. It is not from your Holiness that I learned ecumenism." And Pope John laughed with obvious emotion.

What more can I tell you? The Roman Pontiffs, all of them, have always had understanding and affection for Opus Dei.

Monsignor, I had the opportunity of listening to you answer the questions of an assembly of more than twenty thousand persons gathered in Pamplona a year and a half ago. You insisted then on the need for Catholics to conduct themselves as responsible and free citizens, and

"not to make a living by being Catholic." What impor-
tance and what scope do you give that idea?

I have always been annoyed by the attitude of those who   47
make a profession of calling themselves Catholic, and also of
those who want to deny the principle of personal responsibility, upon which the whole of Christian morality is based.

The spirit of Opus Dei and of its members is to serve the
Church, and all men, without using the Church. I like Catholics to carry Christ not in name, but in their conduct, giving a
real witness of Christian life. I find clericalism repellent and I
understand how, as well as an evil anticlericalism, there also
exists a healthy anticlericalism. It proceeds from love for the
priesthood and opposes the use of a sacred mission for
earthly ends, either by a layman or by a priest. But I do not
think that in this I oppose anyone. In our Work there is no
spirit of monopoly. There is only a desire to cooperate with
all who work for Christ, and with all—Christians or not—
who make of their lives a splendid reality of service.

It remains only to say that the important thing is not so
much the dimension I have given to these ideas, especially
since 1928, but that which the Magisterium of the Church
has given them. Not long ago the Council aroused, in the
poor priest that I am, an emotion which is impossible to
describe. For it reminded all Christians, in the Dogmatic Constitution on the Church, that they must feel their full citizen-
ship in the earthly city—by taking part in all human
undertakings with professional competence and with love for
all men, by seeking that Christian perfection to which they
are called by the simple fact of their Baptism.

What is the Attraction of Opus Dei?

Interview with Tad Szulc (*The New York Times*)
—October 7, 1966

Could you state whether—or to what extent—Opus Dei in Spain has an economic and/or political orientation? If affirmative, could you define it?

48   Opus Dei has no political or economic orientation in Spain or elsewhere. Undoubtedly its members are led by Christ's teachings always to defend personal freedom and the rights of all men—the right to live and work, to be cared for in sickness and old age, the right to marry and have a family and give one's children an education in proportion to their individual talents, and the right to be treated as befits free men and citizens.

The Work, however, does not propose concrete solutions for any economic, political, or cultural problem. Each member is absolutely free to think and act as he sees fit in those fields. In all temporal matters he enjoys the greatest possible freedom. Opus Dei is open to peoples of every political, social, cultural, and economic tendency that a Christian conscience can accept.

I never talk about politics. My mission as a priest is exclusively spiritual. Furthermore, even if I did express an opinion on a temporal question, the members of the Work would be under no obligation to follow it.

Opus Dei's directors can never impose a political or professional criterion on other members. If a member of the Work ever tried to do it, or to use other members for some human end, he would be expelled straightaway, because they would rise in legitimate rebellion. I have never asked anyone who belongs to the Work what party he supports or what political ideas he holds; and I will never do so. It would seem to me a violation of his legitimate freedom. And Opus Dei's directors the world over follow the same rule of conduct.

Nevertheless, I am aware that among the members of the Work, in Spain just as in any other country, all shades of opinion are represented; and I have no objection whatsoever. I respect them all, as I will always respect any temporal decision made by a man who tries to act according to the dictates of his conscience.

This pluralism is not a problem for the Work. Rather, it is a sign of good spirit that bears witness to the legitimate liberty of each individual.

Is it a myth, a half-truth, or a fact that Opus Dei in Spain has become a political and economic power through the positions in the official and business world held by its members?

It is purely and simply an error. The majority of Opus Dei 49 members are of modest means and social position: manual workers, farmers, clerks, housewives, office workers, engineers, teachers, and so on. A much smaller number are engaged in the world of government and business. All of them act exclusively on their own authority. They are fully autonomous in their work and answer personally for their actions.

Opus Dei's aims are strictly spiritual. The only thing it asks of its members, be they socially influential or not, is that they strive to lead a fully Christian life. It never gives them instructions on how to carry out their work. It does not attempt to coordinate their activities; nor does it make use of the positions they may hold.

In this sense, the Work could be compared to a sports club or a charitable institution that is in no way related to the political or economic activities of the people who belong to it.

If, as claimed by its members, Opus Dei is simply a religious association in which each man is free to pursue his own line of thought, how do you explain the widespread belief that Opus Dei is a monolithic organization with well-defined positions in temporal matters?

50   I don't think that opinion is really very widely held. Some of the most authoritative organs of the international press have recognized the pluralism of the members of the Work.

Undeniably, however, there are people who maintain the mistaken opinion you mention. It is possible that some of them have propagated it for reasons of their own even though they know it to be false. In many other cases it may be attributed to inadequate knowledge. Being initially ill-informed, it is not surprising that people who lack sufficient interest in the question to enter into contact with Opus Dei and receive firsthand information, attribute to the Work as such the opinions of a few members.

In any case, no one who is reasonably well-informed on what goes on in Spain can ignore the reality of the pluralism to be found among the members of the Work there. I am sure that you could easily cite many examples.

Another factor may be a subconscious prejudice engendered by a one-party mentality, in politics or in the spiritual sphere. People with this mentality want everyone to think the same way as they do and find it difficult to believe that there are people capable of respecting the liberty of other men. Thus they attribute to Opus Dei the monolithic character of their own groups.

It is generally believed that, as an organization, Opus Dei wields considerable economic power. Since Opus Dei does engage in activities in the field of education, social welfare, and so on, could you explain how Opus Dei runs these activities, i.e., how does it obtain funds, how does it coordinate and use them?

In all countries in which it works, Opus Dei does carry out   51
social, educational, and welfare projects. They are not, however, its main function. Opus Dei's aim is to help men and women to be good Christians, and therefore witnesses of Christ in the midst of their everyday occupations. The activities you mention are directed precisely toward that goal. The effectiveness of all our work is, therefore, based on the grace of God and on a life of prayer, work, and sacrifice. But undoubtedly any activity in the field of education or social welfare needs to make use of a certain amount of money.

Each center is financed in the same way as any other of its type. Student residences, for example, with the room and board of the residents, high schools with the pupils' tuition, agricultural schools with the sale of their products. But these funds are hardly ever sufficient to cover all the expenses of a center, especially considering that the Work's activities are all planned with an apostolic outlook and that the majority of them are designed for people with very limited economic resources, who in many cases pay only a nominal fee for the training they receive.

Another important source of funds is the members of the Work who donate part of the money they earn through their professional work. But most important of all is the generous support of many who do not belong to Opus Dei but want to contribute to these social and educational undertakings. The personnel in charge make an effort to arouse an apostolic zeal and a social concern which will move many people to collaborate actively. Since the centers are run with a high degree of professional competence and are planned to meet real needs of the community, in most cases the response has been very generous. You probably know, for example, that the Association of Friends of the University of Navarre has some twelve thousand members.

The finances of each center are autonomous. They are run on an independent basis and look for ways to find the necessary funds among people interested in their activities.

Would you accept the contention that Opus Dei actually "controls" certain banks, business enterprises, newspapers, and the like? If so, what does "control" mean in this context?

52   There are members of Opus Dei (considerably fewer than some rumors would have it) who work at an executive level in businesses of various kinds. Some manage family concerns they inherited. Others run businesses they themselves started or helped to start. Still others have been placed at the head of companies by the owners, who were convinced of their ability. They have reached the positions they hold by any of the honest ways in which people usually reach them. That is to say that it has nothing to do with their membership in Opus Dei.

Like all the other members of the Work, the business executives who belong to Opus Dei seek to live the spirit of the gospel in the exercise of their profession. This means, in the first place, that they have to be scrupulously just and honest. They endeavor to be honest in their business affairs, paying a just salary to their employees, respecting the rights of the shareholders or owners, fulfilling all the laws. They avoid any type of favoritism with respect to other persons, whether they belong to Opus Dei or not. I feel that favoritism would be contrary not only to the search for holiness, which is the reason for their belonging to Opus Dei, but to the most elementary morality.

I already mentioned the absolute freedom enjoyed by Opus Dei members in their professional work. This implies that the business executives who belong to the Work run their companies as they see fit, without receiving any instructions from Opus Dei's directors as to how they should carry out their work. The economic and financial policies they adopt, and the ideological orientation in the case of a newspaper or other publication, is their exclusive responsibility.

Any attempt to picture Opus Dei as a source of temporal or economic directives is completely unfounded.

How is Opus Dei organized in Spain? How is its leadership constituted and how does it operate? Do you, personally, intervene in the activities in Spain of Opus Dei?

The government of Opus Dei [6] is never in the hands of one individual. Decisions are never taken by a single person. We detest tyranny as opposed to human dignity. In each country the direction of our apostolic activities is entrusted to a commission composed in its majority of laymen of different professions and presided over by the Counselor of Opus Dei in the country. The Counselor in Spain is Dr. Florencio Sánchez Bella.

Since Opus Dei is a supernatural, spiritual organization, its government is limited to directing and orientating its apostolic activities to the exclusion of any temporal end whatsoever. The Work not only respects its members' freedom: it helps them to become fully aware of it. To achieve holiness in their profession or job, Opus Dei members need to be formed in such a way that they can administer their freedom in the presence of God, with sincere piety and with doctrine.

This is the fundamental mission of the directors: to help its members know and practice the Christian faith so they can make it a reality in their lives, with full individual autonomy.

Naturally, in the purely apostolic field a certain degree of coordination is essential, but even there the intervention is limited to the minimum necessary to facilitate the creation of educational and social activities which constitute an effective Christian service.

The principles I just mentioned are also applicable to the central government of Opus Dei. I do not govern alone. Decisions are taken by the General Council of Opus Dei, situated in Rome, made up at present of people from fourteen countries. The General Council limits itself to setting down the basic guidelines for the apostolates of the Work the world over, leaving it up to the directors in each country to put them into effect. The Women's Section is governed in the same way. Its Central Council is made up of women from twelve countries.

Why is Opus Dei, in your opinion, resented by numerous religious orders, such as by the Society of Jesus?

54   I know an immense number of religious who are aware that we are not religious, but who return the affection we harbor for them and pray for our apostolates. With respect to the Society of Jesus, I am personally acquainted with Fr. Arrupe, its Superior General, and can assure you that our relations are of mutual esteem and affection.

You may have met some religious who do not understand or sympathize with our Work. If so, it is probably due to a misunderstanding, or to a lack of knowledge of the specifically secular and lay character of our apostolate, which in no way intrudes on their proper field. We venerate and love all religious, and ask our Lord to make their service to the

Church and to all mankind ever more fruitful. There will never be a dispute between Opus Dei and a religious; it takes two to make an argument, and we have no desire to argue with anyone.

To what do you ascribe the increasing stature of Opus Dei? Is it the appeal of your doctrine in itself or is it also a reflection of the general modern-age anxieties?

Our Lord gave rise to Opus Dei in 1928 to remind Christians 55 that, as we read in the book of Genesis, God created man to work. We have come to call attention once again to the example of Jesus, who spent thirty years in Nazareth working as a carpenter. In his hands, a professional occupation, similar to that carried out by millions of men in the world, was turned into a divine task. It became a part of our redemption, a way to salvation.

The spirit of Opus Dei reflects the marvelous reality (forgotten for centuries by many Christians) that any honest and worthwhile work can be converted into a divine occupation. In God's service there are no second-class jobs; all of them are important.

To love and serve God, there is no need to do anything strange or extraordinary. Christ bids all men without exception to be perfect as his heavenly Father is perfect. Sanctity, for the vast majority of men, implies sanctifying their work, sanctifying themselves in it, and sanctifying others through it. Thus they can encounter God in the course of their daily lives.

The conditions of contemporary society, which places an ever higher value on work, evidently make it easier for the men of our times to understand this aspect of the Christian message that the spirit of the Work has recalled. But even more important is the influence of the Holy Spirit. His vivifying action is making our days the witness of a great movement of renewal in all Christianity. Reading the decrees of the Second Vatican Council, it is clear that an important part of this renewal has been precisely the revaluation of ordinary work and of the dignity of the Christian vocation of life and work in the world.

How is Opus Dei developing in countries other than Spain? What is its influence in the United States, Britain, Italy, and so on?

56 At present, people of sixty-eight nationalities, who work in almost all the countries of America and Western Europe and in various parts of Africa, Asia, and Oceania, belong to Opus Dei.

The influence of Opus Dei in all these countries is a spiritual one. It consists essentially in helping people to live the spirit of the gospel more fully in their everyday lives. The situation of these people is extremely varied—from small farmers who till the land in isolated villages of the Andes to Wall Street bankers. Opus Dei teaches all of them the value of their ordinary work, which can be a highly effective means of loving and serving God and others, be it brilliant or lowly from a human point of view. It teaches them to love all men, to respect their freedom, and to work in the way they personally see fit to eliminate intolerance and make society more just. This is the only influence of Opus Dei in any place where it carries out its apostolates.

On the social and educational undertakings that the Work as such promotes, let me say that they are designed to meet in each locality the concrete needs of society. I do not have at hand detailed information on them for, as I told you earlier, our organization is highly decentralized. I could mention, as one example among many, Midtown Sports and Cultural Center on Chicago's Near North Side, which offers educational and sporting programs to the neighborhood's residents. An important part of its work consists in bringing together in an atmosphere of friendship and collaboration the different ethnic groups that live there. Another interesting activity in the United States is carried out at Tenley Center in Washington, D.C. Its services include professional guidance courses, special studies for gifted students, college preparation programs, and so on.

In England one might mention a number of university residences which provide not only a place to stay but numerous activities to complete students' human, spiritual, and cultural training. Netherhall House in London is perhaps especially interesting because of its marked international character. Students from more than fifty countries have lived there. Many of them are non-Christian, since Opus Dei's houses are open to all without any racial or religious discrimination.

To be brief, I will mention just one more activity, the Centro Internazionale della Gioventu Lavoratrice in Rome. This center for the professional training of young workers was entrusted to Opus Dei by Pope John XXIII and inaugurated by Pope Paul VI.

How do you visualize the future of Opus Dei in the years to come?

Opus Dei is still very young. Thirty-nine years is barely a beginning for an institution. Our aim is to collaborate with all other Christians in the great mission of being witnesses of Christ's gospel, to recall that it can vivify any human situation. The task that awaits us is immense. It is a sea without shores, for as long as there are men on earth, no matter how much the techniques of production may change, they will   57 have some type of work that can be offered to God and sanctified. With God's grace, Opus Dei wants to teach them how to make their work an act of service to all men of every condition, race, and religion. Serving men in this way, they will serve God.

Opus Dei: Fostering the Search for Holiness

Interview with Enrico Zuppi and Antonino Fugardi
(*L'Osservatore della Domenica*)
—published May 19, 26, and June 2, 1968

Opus Dei has played a leading role in the modern development of the laity. We should therefore like to ask you first of all what, in your opinion, are the key characteristics of this development.

I have always thought that the basic characteristic of the development of the laity is a new awareness of the dignity of the Christian vocation. God's call, the character conferred by Baptism, and grace mean that every single Christian can and should be a living expression of the faith. Every Christian should be "another Christ," "Christ himself," present among men. The Holy Father has put it in a way that leaves no room for doubt: "It is necessary to restore to Holy Baptism its full significance. By means of this sacrament we are incorporated into the mystical body of Christ, which is the Church. . . . To be a Christian, to have received Baptism, should not be looked upon as something indifferent or of little importance. It should be imprinted deeply and joyously on the conscience of every baptized person." [1]

This brings with it a deeper awareness of the Church as a community made up of all the faithful, where all share in one and the same mission, which each should fulfill according to his personal circumstances. Lay people, moved by the Holy Spirit, are becoming ever more conscious of the fact that they *are* the Church, that they have a specific and sublime mission

58

59

to which they feel committed because they have been called to it by God himself. And they know that this mission derives from the very fact of their being Christians and not necessarily from a mandate of the hierarchy; although obviously they ought to fulfill it in a spirit of union with the hierarchy and following the teaching authority of the Church. If they are not in union with the bishops and with their head the Pope they cannot, if they are Catholics, be united to Christ.

Lay people have their own way of contributing to the holiness and apostolate of the Church. They do so by their free and responsible action within the temporal sphere, to which they bring the leaven of Christianity. Giving Christian witness in their everyday lives, spreading the word which enlightens in the name of God, acting responsibly in the service of others and thus contributing to the solution of common problems: these are some of the ways in which ordinary Christians fulfill their divine mission.

For many years now, ever since the foundation of Opus Dei, I have meditated and asked others to meditate on those words of Christ which we find in Saint John: "And when I am lifted up from the earth, I shall draw all things to myself" (Jn 12:32). By his death on the Cross, Christ has drawn all creation to himself. Now it is the task of Christians, in his name, to reconcile all things with God, placing Christ, by means of their work in the middle of the world, at the summit of all human activities.

I should like to add that alongside the laity's new awareness of their role there is a similar development among the clergy. They too are coming to realize that lay people have a role of their own which should be fostered and stimulated by pastoral action aimed at discovering the presence in the midst of the People of God of the charism of holiness and apostolate, in the infinitely varied forms in which God bestows it.

This new pastoral approach, though very demanding, is,

to my mind, absolutely necessary. It calls for the supernatural gift of discernment of spirits, for sensitivity toward the things of God, and for the humility of not imposing personal preferences on others and of seconding the inspirations which God arouses in souls. In a word: it means loving the rightful freedom of the sons of God who find Christ, and become bearers of Christ, while following paths which are very diverse but which are all equally divine.

One of the greatest dangers threatening the Church today may well be precisely that of not recognizing the divine requirements of Christian freedom and of being led by false arguments in favor of greater effectiveness to try to impose uniformity on Christians. At the root of this kind of attitude is something not only lawful but even commendable: a desire to see the Church exercising a vital influence on the modern world. However, I very much fear that this is a mistaken way, for on the one hand it can tend to involve and commit the hierarchy in temporal questions (thus falling into a clericalism which, though different, is no less scandalous than that of past centuries), and, on the other hand, to isolate lay people, ordinary Christians, from the everyday world, turning them into mouthpieces for decisions or ideas conceived outside the world in which they live.

I feel we priests are being asked to have *the humility of learning not to be fashionable*; of being in fact servants of the servants of God and making our own the cry of the Baptist: "He must increase, I must decrease" (Jn 3:30), so as to enable ordinary Christians, the laity, to make Christ present in all sectors of society. One of the fundamental tasks of the priest is and always will be to give doctrine, to help individuals and society become aware of the duties the gospel imposes on them, and to move men to discern the signs of the times. But all priestly work should be carried out with the maximum respect for the rightful freedom of consciences:

every man ought to respond to God freely. And besides, every Catholic, as well as receiving help from the priest, also has lights of his own which he receives from God and a grace of state to carry out the specific mission which, as a man and as a Christian, he has received.

Anyone who thinks that Christ's voice will not be heard in the world today unless the clergy are present and speak out on every issue has not yet understood the dignity of the divine vocation of each and every member of the Christian faithful.

In this context, what is the role Opus Dei has fulfilled and is at present fulfilling?

60   It is not for me to evaluate the work which, through the grace of God, Opus Dei has done. All I would say is that the purpose of Opus Dei is to foster the search for holiness and the carrying out of the apostolate by Christians who live in the world, whatever their state in life or position in society.

The Work was born to help those Christians who, through their family, their friendships, their ordinary work, their aspirations, form part of the very texture of civil society, to understand that their life, just as it is, can be an opportunity for meeting Christ: that it is a way of holiness and apostolate. Christ is present in any honest human activity. The life of an ordinary Christian, which to some people may seem banal and petty, can and should be a holy and sanctifying life.

In other words: if you want to follow Christ, to serve the Church and help other men to recognize their eternal destiny, there is no need to leave the world or keep it at arm's length. You don't even need to take up an ecclesiastical activity. The only condition which is both necessary and sufficient is to fulfill the mission which God has given you, in the place and in the environment indicated by his Providence.

Since God wants the majority of Christians to remain in secular activities and to sanctify the world from within, the purpose of Opus Dei is to help them discover their divine mission, showing them that their human vocation—their professional, family, and social vocation—is not opposed to their supernatural vocation. On the contrary, it is an integral part of it.

The one and only mission of Opus Dei is the spreading of this message, which comes from the gospel, among all those who live and work in the world, whatever be their background, profession, or trade. And to those who grasp this ideal of holiness, the Work offers the spiritual assistance and the doctrinal, ascetical, and apostolic training which they need to put it into practice.

Members of Opus Dei do not act as a group. They act individually, with personal freedom and responsibility. Thus Opus Dei is not a "closed organization" or one which in some way gathers its members together to isolate them from the rest of men. The "corporate activities," which are the only ones the Work runs and for which it takes responsibility, are open to everyone with no type of social, cultural, or religious discrimination. And the members, precisely because it is in the world that they seek sanctity, always work with the people with whom they are connected through their job or their participation in civic life.

It is an essential part of the Christian spirit not only to live in union with the ordinary hierarchy—the Pope and the bishops—but also to feel at one with the rest of one's brothers in the faith. For a long time I have thought that one of the worst ills affecting the Church today is the ignorance many Catholics have as regards what Catholics in other countries or sectors of society are doing and thinking. We must rekindle the sense of brotherliness which was so deeply felt by the early Christians. It will help us to feel united, while loving at the same time the variety of our individual vocations. And it will lead us to avoid many of the unjust and offensive judgments made by particular little groups in the name of Catholicism, against their brothers in the faith, who in fact are acting nobly and with a spirit of sacrifice in the particular circumstances of their own countries.

The important thing is for everyone to try to be faithful to his own divine calling. Only thus can he contribute to the Church the benefits deriving from the special charism he has received from God. What members of Opus Dei, who are ordinary Christians, have to do is to sanctify the world from within, taking part in the whole range of human activities. Since their membership in Opus Dei in no way modifies their situation on the world, they take part, as they see fit, in the life of the parish, in group religious celebrations, and so on. In this sense too they are ordinary Christians who want to be good Catholics.

However, the members of the Work do not as a rule take part in confessional activities. Only in exceptional cases, at the express request of the hierarchy, do members of Opus Dei work in ecclesiastical activities. They don't take up this attitude in order to be different and still less out of disregard for confessional activities. It is simply that they want to do what befits the vocation to Opus Dei. There are already many religious and clergy, and many lay people also, who work in these activities and put their wholehearted efforts into them.

The task to which members of the Work are called by God is of another kind. Within the framework of the universal call to holiness, members of Opus Dei receive in addition a special call to dedicate themselves freely and responsibly to look for holiness and carry out the apostolate in the middle of the world, committing themselves to live a particular spirituality and to receive throughout their lives a specific formation. If they were to neglect their work in the world in order to carry out ecclesiastical activities, the divine gifts they have received would be wasted and, through a misguided desire for immediate pastoral effectiveness, they would do real harm to the Church. For there would be fewer Christians dedicated to sanctifying themselves in all the professions and trades of civil society, in the immense field of secular work.

And anyway the demands which continuous religious and professional training make, as well as the time which each individual dedicates to acts of piety, to prayer, and to the generous fulfillment of the duties of his state keep the members fully occupied. There just isn't any spare time.

We know that men and women of all walks of life, single and married people, belong to Opus Dei. What is the common element in the vocation to Opus Dei? What commitments does each member take on in order to attain the aims of Opus Dei?

I can put it in very few words: to look for holiness in the middle of the world, *nel bel mezzo della strada*, as the Italian phrase has it. A person who receives from God the specific vocation to Opus Dei is convinced that he must achieve holiness in his own state in life, in his work, whether it be manual or intellectual, and he lives accordingly. I say he "is convinced . . . and he lives accordingly" because it is not a matter of accepting a simple theoretical proposition, but rather of putting it into practice day after day, in ordinary life.

If you want to achieve holiness—in spite of your personal shortcomings and miseries, which will last as long as you live—you must make an effort, with God's grace, to practice charity, which is the fullness of the law and the bond of perfection. Charity is not something abstract. It entails a real, complete, self-giving to the service of God and all men: to the service of that God who speaks to us in the silence of prayer

62

and in the hubbub of the world and of those men whose existence is interwoven with our own. By living charity— Love—you live all the human and supernatural virtues demanded of a Christian. These virtues form a unity and cannot be reduced to a mere list. You can't have charity without justice, solidarity, family and social responsibility, poverty, joy, chastity, friendship . . .

You can see immediately that the practice of these virtues leads to apostolate. In fact it already is apostolate. For when people try to live in this way in the middle of their daily work, their Christian behavior becomes good example, witness, something which is a real and effective help to others. They learn to follow in the footsteps of Christ, who "began to do and to teach" (Acts 1: 1), joining example with word. That is why, for these past forty years, I have been calling this apostolate an *apostolate of friendship and confidence.*

All the members of Opus Dei have this same desire for holiness and apostolate. And so, in the Work, there are no degrees or categories of membership. The vocation of Opus Dei is one and the same. It is a call to commit oneself personally, freely, and responsibly to try to carry out the will of God, that is what God wants each individual to do. What there is is a multitude of personal situations, the situation of each member in the world, to which the same specific vocation is adapted.

As you can see, the pastoral phenomenon of Opus Dei is something born *from below*, from the everyday lives of Christians who live and work alongside the rest of men. Thus it does not form part of the secularizing process, the "desacralization," of monastic or religious life. It is not a link in the chain which is drawing the religious closer to the world.

When a person receives the vocation to Opus Dei he acquires a new vision of the things around him. He sees his social relationships, his profession, his interests, his sorrows, and his joys in a new light. But not for a moment does he stop living in the midst of them. Thus one cannot speak of adaptation to the world or to modern society. No one adapts himself to what is part and parcel of himself: with respect to what is proper to himself he simply is. His vocation is the same as that which those fishermen, peasants, merchants, or soldiers received in their hearts as they sat at Jesus' feet in Galilee and heard him say: "You must be perfect as your heavenly Father is perfect" (Mt 5:48).

Let me put it this way: the perfection which a member of Opus Dei looks for is the perfection proper to a Christian. It is the same perfection to which every Christian is called, and it consists in living fully the requirements of the faith. We are not interested in "evangelical perfection," which is regarded as proper to the religious and to some institutions set up on religious lines. Still less are we interested in the "life of evangelical perfection," which in Canon Law refers to the *religious state*.

I consider the religious vocation a blessed one and one which the Church needs, and anyone who did not venerate that vocation would not have the spirit of the Work. But it is not my vocation, nor that of the members of Opus Dei. You can say that, in coming to Opus Dei, each and every member has come *on the explicit condition of not changing his state in life*. The specific characteristic of our way is to sanctify one's state of life in the world, and to be sanctified in the place of one's *meeting* with Christ. This is the commitment which each member takes on to attain the aims of Opus Dei.

How is Opus Dei organized?

Since, as I have just said, the vocation to the Work finds a man   63
or a woman in his or her normal life, in the middle of their

work, you can understand that Opus Dei is not built up on the basis of committees, assemblies, meetings, and so on. On occasion, to the surprise of some people, I have gone so far as to say that Opus Dei, in this sense, is an *unorganized organization*. The majority of the members, practically all, in fact, live in the same place as they would have lived had they not been members of Opus Dei: in their home, with their family, in the place where they work.

And it's there precisely that each member of the Work fulfills the purpose of Opus Dei: to try to be holy, making his life a daily apostolate, which is ordinary, insignificant if you like, but persevering and divinely effective. That's the important thing. And to nourish this life of holiness and apostolate they receive from Opus Dei the spiritual help, advice, and orientation they need. But only in the strictly spiritual sphere. In everything else—in their work, in their social relationships, and the like—they act as they wish, knowing that this is not neutral ground but material in which they can be sanctified and which itself can be sanctified and become a means of apostolate.

And so all live their own lives, with the relationships and obligations this entails, and they turn to the Work for spiritual help. This does call for a certain amount of structure, but always a very small amount. Everything is done to limit it to what is strictly indispensable. The Work does organize religious doctrinal training, which lasts all one's life and leads one to an active, sincere, and genuine piety and to an ardor which necessarily encourages constant, contemplative prayer and a personal and responsible apostolic activity, devoid of any kind of fanaticism.

In addition to this, all the members know where they can find a priest of the Work with whom they can discuss matters of conscience. Some members, very few in comparison with the total number, live together to look after the spiritual care of the others or to run some apostolic activity; they form an ordinary home, just like any Christian family, and continue at the same time to work at their profession.

In each country there is a regional government, always collegiate in character, headed by a Counselor; and there is a central government in Rome made up of people of very different nationalities. Opus Dei has two Sections, one for men and one for women, which are absolutely independent, to the extent of forming two distinct associations, united only in the person of the President General.[7]

I hope I have explained what I mean by "unorganized organization": we give priority to spirit over organization, and so the life of the members is not straitjacketed by directives, plans, and meetings. Each member goes his own way. What unites him to the others is a shared spirit and a shared desire for holiness and apostolate which accompany him as he strives to sanctify his own everyday life.

Opus Dei has sometimes been described as an intellectual elite which wants to penetrate key political, financial, and cultural sectors to control them from within, although with good intentions. Is this true?

Almost all the institutions which have brought a new message or have seriously tried to serve mankind by living Christianity fully have met with misunderstanding, especially at the beginning. That's why at the start some people did not understand the doctrine on lay apostolate which Opus Dei lived and proclaimed.

I must also add—although I don't like to talk about these things—that in our case there was also an organized and persistent campaign of misrepresentation. There were people who said we acted secretly (perhaps this was their own line of behavior), that we wanted to occupy important positions,

64

and so on. To be more specific, I can say that this campaign was begun, about thirty years ago, by a Spanish religious who later left his order and the Church. He married in a registry office and is now a Protestant minister. Once misrepresentation starts it is carried along for a time by its own momentum—because there are people who write without checking their information, and then not everyone acts as do competent journalists who, realizing they are not infallible, are honest enough to make amends when they find out the truth. And this is what has happened in this case even though these slanders are contradicted by evidence that is clear to everyone, not to mention the fact that they appear incredible right from the word go. Anyway, all this gossip to which you have referred concerns only Spain, and anyone who thinks that an international organization like Opus Dei gravitates around the problems of one country has a shortsighted and provincial outlook.

The majority of the members of Opus Dei—in Spain and elsewhere—are housewives, workers, shopkeepers, clerks, for example, people whose jobs carry no special political or social weight. The fact that a large number of workers are members of Opus Dei attracts no attention; but one politician, plenty. As far as I'm concerned, the vocation to Opus Dei of a railway porter is as important as that of a company director. It's God who does the calling, and in the works of God there is no room for discrimination and still less if it is based on demagoguery.

Anyone who, on seeing members of Opus Dei working in all the different fields of human activity, thinks only in terms of "influence" and "control," is simply showing what a poor conception of Christian life he has. Opus Dei has no power, and wants no power, over any temporal activity. All it wants is to spread a gospel message, to tell all men who live in the world that God wants them to love him and serve him by, with, and through their secular activities. It follows that the members of Opus Dei, who are ordinary Christians, work wherever and however they like. The only thing the Work does is to help them spiritually, so that they can always act with a Christian conscience.

But let's talk specifically about Spain. The few members of 65 Opus Dei who hold prominent social or political positions in Spain do so—as in all other countries—with personal freedom and responsibility, each following his conscience. That is why in practice you find them taking up very different and not infrequently opposed attitudes.

I should also like to point out that to talk about the presence of members of Opus Dei in Spanish politics as if it were something special gives a very false idea of the facts. For the members of Opus Dei who take part in Spanish public life are a minority as compared with the number of Catholics who are actively involved in that area. Since practically the whole population of the country is Catholic, statistical logic leads one to expect that the people who take part in public life should also be Catholics. In fact, you can find at all levels of public administration—from the ministries to the local town councils—plenty of Catholics from all sorts of associations of the faithful: some branches of Catholic Action, the ACNP (the National Catholic Association of Propagandists, whose first president was the late Cardinal Herrera), the Sodalities of our Lady, and so on.

I don't want to go any further into this subject, but I would like to take this opportunity to state once more that Opus Dei is bound up with no country, no government, no political party, nor with any ideology. In temporal questions its members always act with full freedom and shoulder the responsibility for their actions. They abominate any attempt to make use of religion to support political or party interests.

Simple things are sometimes difficult to explain. That's

why I have given you a rather long answer. Anyway the sort of gossip you refer to is now a thing of the past. These slanders have long stood discredited: now no one believes them. From the very beginning we have always acted in the full light of day (there was no reason for acting otherwise), giving a clear explanation of the nature and aims of our apostolate. Anyone who wanted the facts has always been able to get them. The truth of the matter is that very many people—Catholics and non-Catholics, Christians and non-Christians—regard our work with affection and esteem and cooperate in it.

66   It is also true that progress in the history of the Church has led to the disappearance of a certain kind of clericalism which tended to misconstrue everything which lay people did and to regard their activity as double-faced and hypocritical. Thanks to this progress it is easier nowadays to understand that what Opus Dei has lived and proclaimed was purely and simply the divine vocation of the ordinary Christian, with a precise supernatural commitment.

I hope the time will come when the phrase "the Catholics are penetrating all sectors of society" will go out of circulation because everyone will have realized that it is a clerical expression. In any event, it is quite inapplicable to the apostolate of Opus Dei. The members of the Work have no need to "penetrate" the temporal sector for the simple reason that they are ordinary citizens, the same as their fellow citizens, and so they are there already.

When God calls someone who works in a factory or a hospital or in parliament to Opus Dei, it means that person henceforward will be determined to avail of the means necessary for sanctifying his job, with the grace of God. In other words, he has become aware of the radical demands of the gospel message, as they apply to the specific vocation he has received.

To deduce that this awareness means leaving normal life is

a conclusion that is only valid for people who receive from God a religious vocation, with its *contemptus mundi*, its disdain for the things of the world. But to try to make this abandonment of the world the quintessence or summit of Christianity would obviously be absurd.

So it's not that Opus Dei puts its members into particular environments. They are, I repeat, already there, and there's no reason why they should leave. Moreover, vocations to Opus Dei, which come through God's grace and through that apostolate of friendship and confidence which I mentioned earlier, are to be found in all environments.

Perhaps this very simplicity of the nature and way of working of Opus Dei presents a difficulty for people who are full of complications and seem incapable of understanding anything genuine and upright,

Naturally, there will always be some people who do not understand the essence of Opus Dei, but this should come as no surprise because our Lord gave his disciples a forewarning of these difficulties when he told them: "No disciple is above his master" (Mt 10:24). No one can hope to be understood by everyone, although he does have a right to be respected as a person and as a son of God. Unfortunately, there are always some fanatics who want to impose their own ideas in a totalitarian way, and these will never grasp the love which the members of Opus Dei have for the personal freedom of others and then also for their own personal freedom, which is always accompanied by personal responsibility.

I remember a very graphic anecdote. In a particular city which will remain anonymous, the corporation was debating a grant of money for an educational activity run by members of Opus Dei—which, like all the corporate activities fostered by the Work, was making a definite contribution to the good of the community. Most of the councilors were in favor of the grant. One of them, a socialist, explained his opinion, saying that he knew the activity personally: "This is an activity," he said, "which is characterized by the fact that the people who run it are good friends of personal freedom: students of all religions and ideologies are welcomed in the residence." The communist councilors voted against the grant. One of them, saying why he did so, told the socialist: "I am opposed to it because if that's the way things are, this residence is doing effective propaganda for Catholicism."

Anyone who does not respect the freedom of others or wants to oppose the Church is incapable of appreciating an apostolic activity. But even in such a case I, as a man, am obliged to respect him and to try to lead him to the truth; and as a Christian, I must love him and pray for him.

Thank you for clarifying that point. I should like to ask you now what characteristics of the spiritual formation of the members make it impossible for anyone to derive any temporal advantage from belonging to Opus Dei?

67   Any advantage which is not exclusively spiritual is completely ruled out, because the Work *demands a great deal*—detachment, sacrifice, self-denial, unceasing work in the service of souls—and *gives nothing*. Nothing, that is, in terms of material advantages; because in the spiritual sphere it gives very much. It offers the means to fight and win in the ascetical struggle. It leads one along ways of prayer. It teaches one to treat Jesus as a brother, to see God in all the circumstances of one's life, to see oneself as a son of God and therefore to feel committed to spreading his teaching.

Anyone who does not progress along the way of the interior life, to the extent of realizing it's worthwhile to give oneself in everything, will find it impossible to persevere in Opus Dei, because holiness is not just a nice-sounding phrase to be bandied about; it's a very demanding affair.

And besides, Opus Dei has no activity with political, financial, or ideological aims. It has no temporal action. Its only activities are the supernatural formation of its members and the works of apostolate—in other words, the constant spiritual attention it gives to the members and the corporate apostolic undertakings in the areas of social welfare, education, and so on.

The members of Opus Dei have come together *only* for the purpose of following a clearly defined way of holiness and of cooperating in specific works of apostolate. What binds them together is something exclusively spiritual and therefore rules out all temporal interests, because in the temporal area all the members of Opus Dei are free and so each goes his own way, with aims and interests which are different and sometimes opposite.

Because the Work's aims are exclusively supernatural, its spirit is one of freedom, of love for the personal freedom of all men. And since this is a sincere love for freedom and not a mere theoretical statement, we love the necessary consequence of freedom, which is pluralism. In Opus Dei pluralism is not simply tolerated. It is desired and loved, and in no way hindered. When I see among the members of the Work so many different ideas, such a variety of points of view in political, economic, social, or cultural matters, I am overjoyed at the sight, because it's a sign that everything is being done for God, as it should be.

Spiritual unity is compatible with variety in temporal matters when extremism and intolerance are shunned and above all when people live up to the faith and realize that men are united not so much by links of sympathy or mutual interest but above all by the action of the one Spirit, who in making us brothers of Christ is leading us toward God the Father.

A true Christian never thinks that unity in the faith,

fidelity to the teaching authority and tradition of the Church, and concern for the spreading of the saving message of Christ run counter to the existence of variety in the attitudes of people as regards the things which God has left, as the phrase goes, to the free discussion of men. In fact, he is fully aware that this variety forms part of God's plan. It is something desired by God, who distributes his gifts and his lights as he wishes. The Christian should love other people and therefore respect opinions contrary to his own, and live in harmony and full brotherhood with people who do not think as he does.

Precisely because this is the spirit which the members of the Work have learnt, none of them would dream of using the fact that he belongs to Opus Dei to obtain any personal advantage or to try to impose his political or cultural opinions on the others: they just wouldn't put up with it, and they would ask him to change his attitude or leave the Work. This is a point on which no one in Opus Dei can ever permit the least deviation, because it is their duty to defend not only their own freedom but also the supernatural character of the activity to which they have dedicated their lives. That's why I think that personal freedom and responsibility are the best guarantee of the supernatural purpose of the Work of God.

It could perhaps be said that so far Opus Dei has benefited from the enthusiasm of its first members, although admittedly there are many thousands of them now. Is there any way of guaranteeing the continuity of the Work against the risk, which all institutions run, of a possible cooling down of the initial fervor and drive?

68   The Work is based not on enthusiasm but on faith. The early years were long years, and they were very hard. All we could

see before us were difficulties. Opus Dei went ahead by the grace of God and by the prayer and sacrifice of the first few, despite the lack of material resources. All we had was youth, good humor, and a desire to do God's will.

From the beginning, Opus Dei's weapons have always been prayer, self-giving, and silent renunciation of all forms of selfishness for the sake of serving souls. As I said before, people come to Opus Dei to receive a spirit which brings them to give themselves in everything, while they continue with their ordinary work out of love of God and through him, out of love for men.

The guarantee against any cooling-down is that my sons and daughters should never lose this spirit. I fully realize that human undertakings get worn out with time, but this doesn't happen to divine undertakings unless men debase them. Corruption and decay come only when the divine impetus is lost. In our case one can see clearly the Providence of the Lord which—in so short a time, forty years—has seen to it that this specific divine vocation should be received and lived by ordinary people (they're just the same as their fellow men) in so many different countries.

The aim of Opus Dei is, I insist once again, the holiness of each one of its members, men and women who carry on just where they were before they joined the Work. All who come to Opus Dei must come with the determination to become saints in spite of everything—that is, in spite of their own miseries, their personal shortcomings—otherwise they will go away immediately. I think that holiness attracts holiness, and I pray to God that in Opus Dei there will always be this profound conviction, this life of faith. As you can see, our confidence is not based on merely human or legal guarantees. Undertakings inspired by God move at the pace of divine grace and in these my one and only recipe is this: to be saints, to want to become saints, with personal sanctity.

Why are there priests in an institution so markedly lay as Opus Dei? Can any member of Opus Dei become a priest, or only those who are chosen by the directors?

69   Any person who wants to sanctify his own state in life can receive a vocation to Opus Dei: be he single, married, or widowed; be he layman or cleric.

Diocesan priests therefore can also join Opus Dei. They remain diocesan priests just as they were before, because the Work helps them to tend toward the Christian perfection proper to their state, through the sanctification of their ordinary work, which consists precisely in the priestly ministry at the service of their own bishop, of the diocese, and of the whole Church. In their case also their commitment to Opus Dei in no way changes their position. They remain fully dedicated to the tasks entrusted to them by their bishop and to the other apostolates and activities for which they are responsible—the Work never interferes in these activities. They sanctify themselves by practicing as perfectly as they can the virtues proper to priests.

As well as these priests who join Opus Dei after having received Holy Orders, there are in the Work other secular priests who receive the sacrament after coming to Opus Dei, which they joined as lay people, ordinary Christians. These are very few in comparison with the total number of members, less than two percent, and they devote themselves to serving the apostolic aims of Opus Dei by means of their sacred ministry, giving up more or less, depending on the case, the exercise of their civil profession. They are, in effect, professional people or workers who are called to the priesthood after having become professionally qualified and after years of work at their jobs, as doctors, engineers, mechanics, farm workers, teachers, journalists, and so forth. As well as this they study the relevant ecclesiastical subjects, calmly and thoroughly, and do an ecclesiastical doctorate, and all this without losing the outlook characteristic of their own profession or occupation.

Their presence is needed in the apostolate of Opus Dei. This apostolate is carried out basically by the lay people, as I have said. Each member strives to be an apostle in his own environment, bringing people closer to Christ by his example and word, by dialogue. But in the apostolate, in bringing souls along the paths of the interior life, they come up against the "sacramental wall." The sanctifying role of the lay person is incomplete without the sanctifying role of the priest, who administers the sacrament of Penance, celebrates the Eucharist, and proclaims the word of God in the name of the Church. And since the apostolate of Opus Dei presupposes a specific spirituality, the priest must himself be a living witness to this particular spirit.

As well as serving the other members of the Work, these priests can and in fact do serve many other people. The priestly zeal which permeates their life should lead them to let no one pass by without receiving something of the light of Christ. Furthermore, the spirit of Opus Dei, which will have nothing to do with cliques or discrimination, prompts them to feel intimately and effectively united to their brothers, the other diocesan priests. They feel themselves to be, and in fact are, diocesan priests in all the dioceses where they work and which they try to serve wholeheartedly and effectively.

I should like to stress, because it is very important, that the lay members of Opus Dei who receive Holy Orders do not change their vocation. When they freely accept the invitation of the directors of the Work to become priests, they do not act with the idea of uniting themselves more closely to God or of tending more effectively to holiness. They know perfectly well that the lay vocation is full and complete in itself, that their dedication to God in Opus Dei was right from the start a clear way to achieve Christian perfection. Ordination therefore can in no way be regarded as a crowning of a vocation to Opus Dei: it is simply a calling given to a few people so that they can serve the others in a new way. And then, of course, in the Work there are not two classes of members, priests and lay people. All are, and feel themselves to be, equal; and all live the same spirit: sanctification in one's own state in life.[8]

You have spoken a lot about work. What place would you say work occupies in the spirituality of Opus Dei?

70   Vocation to Opus Dei in no way changes or modifies a person's condition or state in life. And since man's condition, his lot, is to work, the supernatural vocation to holiness and apostolate according to the spirit of Opus Dei confirms this human vocation to work. The immense majority of the members of the Work are lay people, ordinary Christians. Their condition consists in having a profession or trade which is often absorbing and by means of which they earn their living, support their family, contribute to the common good, and develop their own personality.

Vocation to Opus Dei confirms all this: to such an extent that one of the essential signs of this vocation is precisely a determination to remain in the world and to do a job as perfectly as possible (taking into account, of course, one's personal imperfections), and that both from the human and from the supernatural point of view. This means it must be a job which contributes effectively toward both the building up of the earthly city—and therefore it must be done competently and in a spirit of service—and to the consecration of the world—and on this score it must both sanctify and be sanctified.

Those who want to live their faith perfectly and do apostolate according to the spirit of Opus Dei must sanctify themselves with their work, must sanctify their work, and sanctify others through their work. It is while they work alongside their equals, their fellow working men from whom they are in no way different, that they strive to identify themselves with Christ, imitating his thirty years in the workshop at Nazareth.

Ordinary work is not only the context in which they should become holy: it is the *raw material* of their holiness. It is there in the ordinary happenings of their day's work that they discover the hand of God and find the stimulus for their life of prayer. This same professional job brings them into contact with other people—relatives, friends, colleagues— and with the great problems which affect their society and the world at large; and it affords them the opportunity to live that self-giving in the service of others which is essential for Christians. This is where they should strive to give a true and genuine witness to Christ so that all may get to know and love our Lord and discover that their normal life in the world, their everyday work, can be an encounter with God.

In other words, holiness and apostolate and the ordinary life of the members of the Work come to form one and the same thing, and that is why work is the hinge of their spiritual life. Their self-giving to God is grafted on to the work which they were doing before they came to Opus Dei and which they continue to do after they join.

In the early years of my pastoral work, when I began to preach these ideas, some people did not understand me, and others were scandalized: they were so accustomed to hearing the world talked about in a pejorative way. Our Lord had made me understand, and I tried to make other people understand, that the world is good, for the works of God are always perfect, and that it is we men who make the world bad, through our sins.

I said then, as I do now, that we must love the world, because it is in the world that we meet God: God shows himself, he reveals himself to us in the happenings and events of the world.

Good and evil are mixed in human history, and therefore the Christian should be a man of judgment. But this judgment should never bring him to deny the goodness of God's works. On the contrary, it should bring him to recognize the hand of God working through all human actions, even those which betray our fallen nature. You could make a good motto for the Christian life out of these words of Saint Paul: "All things are yours; and you are Christ's; and Christ is God's" (1 Cor 3: 22), and so carry out the plans of that God whose will it is to save the world.

Could you fill me in on the expansion of the Work during the past forty years? What are its most important apostolic activities?

71   I must say, first of all, that I thank God our Lord for letting me see the Work spread throughout the world only forty years after its beginning. When it was born—in Spain, in 1928—it was born *Roman* (which to me means catholic, universal). And its first aim was, inevitably, to spread to all countries.

Looking back on these years I recall a number of things which make me very happy—bound up with the difficulties which are in some way the salt of life. I think of the efficacy of God's grace and the cheerful self-giving of so many men and women who have kept faith. For, I want to stress that the essential apostolate of Opus Dei is the apostolate each member carries out in his own place of work, with his family, among his friends—an apostolate which does not attract attention, which cannot easily be expressed in statistics but which yields holiness in thousands of souls who keep on following Christ, quietly and effectively during their ordinary everyday work.

There is nothing more I can say on this subject. I could tell you about the exemplary lives of so many people—but if I did that I would take away the intimacy and destroy the human and divine creativity of these lives: to reduce it to statistics would be even worse and a waste of time, because the fruit of grace cannot be measured.

But I can add something about the apostolic activities the members of the Work run in different parts of the world—activities with spiritual aims in which they try to work with dedication and with *human perfection also*, and in which so many other people also cooperate: they may not be members of the Work but they appreciate the supernatural value of this activity—or its human value, as in the case of so many people who are not Christians and are such an effective help. These are always lay, secular activities, the initiative of ordinary citizens using their civic rights in accordance with the law of the country; and they are always tackled in a professional way. In other words, they in no way depend on privilege or special favor.

I am sure you know one of the projects of this kind being carried out in Rome: the ELIS Center, which gives technical and general human training to young people by means of schools, sports, cultural activities, libraries, and so forth. It is an activity which meets needs in Rome and in particular in the Tiburtino area. The same sort of thing is being done in Chicago, Madrid, Mexico, and many other places.

Another example is Strathmore College of Arts and Sciences in Nairobi—a pre-university high school which has served hundreds of students from Kenya, Uganda, and Tanzania. Through this college a number of Kenyans in Opus Dei, together with fellow citizens, are doing very useful work in the educational field; it was the first educational establishment in East Africa which brought about complete racial integration—and through its work it has contributed much to the Africanization of culture. Kianda College, also on Nairobi, is a similar enterprise, devoted to the education of young women. Just to take one more, I should like to mention the University of Navarre. Since it was founded in 1952 it has developed eighteen faculties and institutes, with a student enrollment of over six thousand. Contrary to some newspaper reports, the University of Navarre has not been supported by State aid. The Spanish State has contributed nothing to maintenance costs—all it has done is give some subventions to increase the enrollment. The University survives thanks to the help of private individuals and associations. Its teaching system and the pattern of its university life, which are a function of personal responsibility and solidarity of all who take part in the University, have provided valuable experience in the light of the situation of universities today.

I could refer to other kinds of activities in the United States, Japan, Argentine, Australia, the Philippines, Ireland, France, and so forth. But I don't think it is necessary: it is enough to say simply that Opus Dei is today spread to the five continents and that it is comprised of people of over seventy nationalities, of all races and backgrounds.

Finally, are you satisfied with these forty years of activity? Has the experience of recent years (social changes, the Second Vatican Council, and so on) by any chance suggested any changes in the structure of Opus Dei?

72   Satisfied? I cannot but be satisfied, when I see that, despite my own wretchedness, our Lord built up so many wonderful things around this Work of God. The life of a man who lives by faith will always be the story of the mercies of God. At some moments the story may perhaps be difficult to read,

because everything can seem useless and even a failure. But at other times our Lord lets one see how the fruit abounds, and then it is natural for one's soul to break out in thanksgiving.

Indeed, one of my greatest joys was to see the Second Vatican Council so clearly proclaim the divine vocation of the laity. Without any boasting, I would say that as far as our spirit is concerned the Council has not meant an invitation to change but, on the contrary, has confirmed what, with the grace of God, we have been living and teaching for so many years. The principal characteristic of Opus Dei is not a set of techniques or methods of apostolate, not any specific structures, but a spirit which moves one to sanctify one's ordinary work.

As I have repeated on so many occasions, we all have personal shortcomings and miseries. And all of us should seriously examine ourselves in God's presence and check to see how our life measures up to our Lord's demands. But we should not forget the most important thing: "If only you knew the gift of God!" as Jesus said to the Samaritan woman (Jn 4: 10). And Saint Paul adds: "We carry this treasure in earthenware jars, to show that the abundance of the power is God's and not ours" (2 Cor 4: 7).

Humility, Christian self-examination, begins with recognizing God's gift. It is something quite distinct from shrugging one's shoulders at the way things are going. And it has nothing to do with a sense of futility or discouragements in the face of history. In one's personal life, and sometimes also in the life of associations or institutions, there may be things which have to change, perhaps a lot of things. But the attitude with which a Christian should face these problems should be above all one of amazement at the greatness of the works of God, compared with the littleness of man.

Aggiornamento should take place, principally, in one's

114 Conversations with Saint Josemaría Escrivá

personal life so as to bring it into line with the "old novelty" of the gospel. Being up to date means identifying oneself with Christ, who is not a figure of the past—Christ is living and will live for all ages: "Yesterday and today and forever" (Heb 13:8).

Taking Opus Dei as a whole it can be said without any kind of arrogance, but with gratitude to the goodness of God, that it will never have any problems of adaptation to the world: it will never find itself in need of being brought *up to date*.

God our Lord put Opus Dei *up to date* once and for all when he gave the Work its particular lay characteristics. It will never need to adapt itself to the world, because all its members are *of the world*. It will never be forced to catch up with human progress because it is the members of the Work, together with all the other people who live in the world, who make human progress, by means of their *ordinary work*.

The University: At the Service of Society

Interview with Andrés Garrigó (*Gaceta Universitaria*)
—published October 5, 1967

Monsignor Escrivá, we would like to hear your opinion on the essential purpose of a university. In what sense do you feel that the teaching of religion is a part of university studies?

As university students you undoubtedly realize that a university must play a primary role in contributing to human progress. Since the problems facing mankind are multiple and complex (spiritual, cultural, social, financial, and so on) university education must cover all these aspects.   73

A desire to work for the common good is not enough. The way to make this desire effective is to form competent men and women who can transmit to others the maturity which they themselves have achieved.

Religion is the greatest rebellion of men who do not want to live as beasts, who are not satisfied and will not rest until they reach and come to know their Creator. Thus, the study of religion is a fundamental need: a man who lacks religious training is a man whose education is incomplete. That is why religion should be present in the universities, where it should be taught at the high, scholarly level of good theology. A university from which religion is absent is an incomplete university: it neglects a fundamental facet of human personality, which does not exclude but rather presupposes the other facets.

On the other hand, no one may violate the freedom of students' consciences. Religion has to be studied voluntarily, even though Christians know that, if they want to live their faith well, they have a grave obligation to receive a sound religious training. A Christian needs doctrine so as to be able to live by it and to give witness of Christ with example and word.

These days one of the more debated questions is that of democratizing education to make it accessible to all social classes. No one today can imagine an institution of higher education which does not have a social impact or function. How do you understand this process and how can the universities fulfill their social function?

74   A university must educate its students to have a sense of service to society, promoting the common good with their professional work and their activity. University people should be responsible citizens with a healthy concern for the problems of other people and a generous spirit which brings them to face these problems and to resolve them in the best possible way. It is the task of the universities to foster these attitudes in their students.

Everyone who has sufficient ability should have access to higher education, no matter what his social background, economic means, race, or religion. As long as there remain barriers in these areas, democratic education will be little more than an empty phrase.

In a word, the universities should be open to all and should educate their students so that their future professional work may be of service to all.

Many students feel personally involved in world problems and thus want to take an active part in assisting the many people who suffer physically or morally or who are living in poverty. What social ideals would you suggest to the university students of our day?

The ideal I would propose is above all one of work well done   75
and of adequate intellectual preparation during their college
years. Given this basis, there are thousands of places in the
world which need a helping hand, which await someone
who is willing to work personally with effort and sacrifice. A
university should not form men who will egoistically con-
sume the benefits they have achieved through their studies.
Rather, it should prepare students for a life of generous help
to their neighbor, of Christian charity.

Frequently students' concern for social problems is limited to oral or written demonstrations, and at times it degen-
erates into useless or harmful outbursts. I myself measure
the sincerity of concern for others in terms of works of service, and I know of thousands of cases of students in many
countries who have refused to build their own little private
worlds. They are giving themselves to others through their
professional work, which they try to carry out with human
perfection, through educational endeavors, through social
and welfare activities, in a spirit of youth and cheerfulness.

In the context of the present socio-political situation in
our country and in others, or of war, injustice, or
oppression, what responsibility do you attribute to the
university as a corporate body, and to professors and
students? Should a university permit students and
professors to carry on political activities within its
precincts?

First of all, I would like to say that in this conversation I am   76
expressing opinions of my own. Since I was sixteen—and I
am now sixty-five—I have never lost contact with the university, but I am expressing my own personal way of seeing
this matter, and not the point of view of Opus Dei. In temporal and debatable matters Opus Dei does not wish to have

and cannot have any opinion, since its goals are exclusively spiritual. In all matters of free discussion, each member of the Work has and freely expresses his own personal opinion, for which he is also personally responsible.

In reply to your question, I think we would in the first place have to come to an agreement about what we mean by "politics." If by politics we mean being interested in and working for peace, social justice, the freedom of all men, then in that case everyone in the university as a corporate body is obliged to respect those ideals and to foster a concern for resolving the great problems of human life.

But if on the contrary we understand by politics a particular solution to a specific problem, in competition with those who stand for other possible and legitimate solutions, then I think that the university is not the place where politics should be decided.

College years are a period of *preparation* to find solutions for these problems. Everyone should be welcome in the university. It should be a place of study and friendship, a place where people who hold different opinions—which in each period are expressions of the legitimate pluralism which exists in society—may live together in peace.

Supposing that the political circumstances of a country reached such a point that a lecturer or a student thought in conscience that there was no other licit means of preserving the country from general harm, would he be justified in bringing politics into the university in legitimate use of his freedom?

77   In a country in which there were absolutely no political freedom, universities might lose their proper nature, thus ceasing to be the home of all and becoming a battlefield of opposing factions.

Nevertheless, I still think it would be preferable to spend one's college years acquiring a sound training and a social conscience, so that those who govern later on (those who today are studying) will not fall into the same aversion to personal freedom, which is something really pathological. If the universities are turned into a debating hall for the solution of specific political problems, academic serenity will easily be lost and students will develop a partisan outlook. Thus the universities and the country would always suffer from the chronic illness of totalitarianism, of one kind or another.

Let it be clear that, when I say universities are not the place for politics, I do not exclude, but rather desire, a normal channel of opinion for all citizens. Although my opinion in this matter is very definite, I do not wish to add any more because my mission is not political but priestly. What I say to you is something which I have a right to speak about because I consider myself a university man: I have a passionate interest in everything which refers to university life. I do not act in politics. I do not wish to, and I cannot. But my outlook as a jurist and theologian, and my Christian faith, lead me always to stand up for the legitimate freedom of all men.

No one has a right to impose non-existent dogmas in temporal matters. Given a concrete problem, whichever it may be, the solution is to study it well and then to act conscientiously, with personal freedom and with personal responsibility as well.

What in your opinion is the role of student associations and unions? What should be the nature of their relations with the academic authorities?

You are asking my opinion on a very broad question. Therefore I am not going to go into details and will deal just with a   78 few general points. I think student associations should intervene in matters which refer specifically to the university. There should be some representatives, freely elected by their fellow students, who are in contact with the academic authorities and who realize that they must work together in a common task. Here they have another opportunity to perform a real service.

You need a statute in order to carry out this common task in a reasonable way, with justice and with efficiency. Matters for discussion must be carefully studied and thought out. If the suggested solutions are properly studied and have been formed in a constructive spirit and not with a desire to create divisions, they acquire authority and come to be accepted on their own merits.

To achieve this, the representatives of student associations need a sound education. First of all, they should respect and cherish the freedom of others, and then their own freedom, with its corresponding responsibilities. Moreover, they should not desire personal publicity nor seek powers to which they have no right. Rather they should seek the good of the university, which is the good of their fellow students. And, finally, the electors should choose their representatives for these qualities and not for reasons which are foreign to the efficacy of their university. Only thus will the university be a home of serene and noble scholarship, which will further the study and formation of all.

Who do you think should have the right to found centers of higher education and under what circumstances? What powers should the State reserve for itself in higher education? Do you consider autonomy a basic principle for the organization of university education? Could you indicate the broad lines along which an autonomous system should be based?

The right to found educational centers is only one aspect of   79
freedom in general. I consider personal freedom necessary
for everyone and in everything that is morally lawful. Hence,
every person or association in a position to do so should have
the possibility of founding centers of education under equal
conditions and without unnecessary obstacles.

The function of the State depends upon the social situation, and this will differ from Germany to England, from Japan
to the United States, to mention countries with very different
educational systems. The State has clear duties in terms of
encouragement, control, and supervision of education. And
this demands equality of opportunity for both private and
State undertakings. To supervise is neither to obstruct, nor to
impede or restrict freedom.

That is why I consider autonomy in teaching necessary:
autonomy is another way of saying academic freedom. The
university, as a corporate whole, must have the independence of an organ in a living body. That is, it must have
freedom within its specific task of service to the common
good. Some of the signs of an effective autonomy could be
these: the freedom to select its professors and administrative
staff; the freedom to establish its curricula; scope for building
up and administering its own endowment: in a word, all the
necessary conditions for a university to be able to lead its
own life, as a service to society as a whole.

*An ever-increasing weight of criticism is being leveled by
student opinion against lifelong appointments to university posts. Do you think this current of opinion is correct?*

Yes. Although I recognize the high academic and personal   80
standards of the teaching body in this country, I prefer the
free contract system. I think that this system does no financial
harm to the member of staff and that it is an incentive for him

never to give up research or progress in his speciality. Also, it prevents people from understanding university appointments as fiefs, rather than as positions of service.

I realize that the system of permanent university appointments may give good results in some countries, and that within this system you can find very competent men who turn their appointments into a very real service to the university. But I consider that the free contract system makes those cases more frequent and helps to stimulate all professors to dedicate all their energies to the service of the university.

Don't you think that after Vatican II the concepts of "Church schools," "Catholic schools," "Church universities," for example, have become outdated? Don't you think that such titles involve the Church unduly and sound like privileges?

81   No, I don't think so, if by Church schools, Catholic schools, and so on, we understand the results of the rights which the Church and the religious orders and congregations have to create centers of education. To set up a school or a university is not a privilege but a burden; that is, if you try to make it a center for everyone and not only for people with means.

The Council did not intend to declare that confessional centers of teaching were outdated. It simply wanted to make clear that there is another way (which is also more necessary and universal, and which has been lived for many years by the members of Opus Dei) for Christians to be present in the field of education: the free initiative of Catholic citizens who are teachers by profession and who work both in State schools and private centers. This is one more sign of the Church's awareness at the present time of the fruitfulness of the apostolate of the laity.

On the other hand, I must confess that I do not like the

expressions "Catholic schools," "Church schools," and so forth, even though I respect those who think differently. I prefer to see things distinguished by their results and not by their names. A school is truly Christian when it strives for excellence and gives a complete education—which includes Christian ideals—while at the same time respecting personal freedom and earnestly furthering social justice. If this is accomplished, then the name is of little importance. Personally, I repeat, I prefer to avoid those adjectives.

We would like you, as the chancellor of the University of Navarre, to outline the principles which moved you to found it and to explain its significance today in relation to higher education in Spain.

The University of Navarre was founded in 1952—after many years of prayer, I am happy to say—with the idea of being a university which would express the cultural and apostolic ideals of a group of professors who felt deeply about education. It aimed then, as it does today, to contribute side by side with the other universities to solve a serious educational problem in Spain and in many other countries, which need men who are well-trained in order to build a more just society.   82

Those who began it were no strangers to the Spanish university scene. They were professors who had been educated and had taught at Madrid, Barcelona, Seville, Santiago, Granada, and many other universities. This close cooperation, which I venture to say was closer even than that between neighboring State universities, still continues. There are frequent interchanges and visits by professors, and national congresses where work is carried out in harmony, and so on. The same contact has been maintained with the best universities in other countries. The present conferring of honorary degrees on professors of the Sorbonne, of Harvard, Coimbra, Munich, and Louvain is an expression of this close contact.

The University of Navarre has stimulated the contributions to higher education of many people who consider that university studies open to all who deserve to study, regardless of their financial resources, are basic to progress. The Association of Friends of the University of Navarre, with its generous help, has distributed a considerable number of scholarships and grants. This number will continue to increase, as will the number of Afro-Asian and Latin-American students.

It has been said that the University of Navarre is a university for people with means and that nevertheless it receives considerable support from the State. We know the first part is not true because we know our fellow students; but what about the State subsidies?

83   The facts have been made available to the public through the press. They show that, while its fees are approximately the same as those of other universities, the University of Navarre gives financial aid to more students than does any other university in the country. And I can assure you the number of scholarships will be increased further. We aim to reach a percentage of scholarship holders as high, if not higher, than that registered by the non-Spanish universities, which are most outstanding in their efforts to help students.

I can understand that Navarre attracts attention because it functions very efficiently, and this makes people speculate about the existence of massive financial resources. But they forget, when they reason that way, that material resources are not sufficient in themselves to make an institution prosper. The vitality of this university is due principally to the sense of service, the enthusiasm, and the effort which its teaching staff, students, employees, and the admirable women of Navarre who do the cleaning have put into it. If it were not for their efforts, the university would not have been able to keep going.

Financially, the university is supported by subsidies. In the first instance, that of the Provincial Council of Navarre, which is for operating expenses. One must also mention the grant of land for the university buildings made by the Pamplona City Council, following a common practice of city councils in many countries. You know from experience the cultural and economic advantages which a region like Navarre and in particular the city of Pamplona derive from a modern university which opens to all the possibility of receiving good higher education.

You ask about State subsidies. The Spanish government gives no help for the operating expenses of the University of Navarre. It has granted some subsidies for the buildings necessary to accommodate larger numbers of students, which alleviate the great financial effort which the university has to make to set up these new facilities.

Other sources of income (for the School of Industrial Engineering) are the Corporations in Guipozcoa and particularly the Provincial Bank of Guipozcoa.

From the start the help given by Spanish and foreign foundations, both public and private, has played an important role. For example, a large official grant from the United States for scientific equipment for the School of Industrial Engineering; the contribution from the German foundation *Misereor* toward the new buildings; the help from the Huarte Foundation for cancer research; grants from the Gulbenkian Foundation; and on and on.

Then there is the help for which we are, if it were possible, even more grateful: that of the thousands of people in

Spain and abroad, of all social classes, who are cooperating insofar as they can to maintain the University, even though many of them have very limited financial means.

Finally, one must not forget those companies whose interest leads them to cooperate in the research carried out by the University or to help in some other way.

You might imagine that with all this there is money to spare. Well, it isn't so. The University of Navarre still runs a deficit. I would like still more people and more foundations to help so that this work of service and social welfare can continue and expand.

As the founder of Opus Dei and the force behind a wide range of university-level educational centers all over the world, could you tell us both why Opus Dei has started these centers and what are the principal features of its contribution to this level of teaching?

84   The aim of Opus Dei is that many people all over the world should come to know both in theory and in practice that it is possible to sanctify their ordinary tasks, their daily work; that it is possible to seek Christian perfection in the middle of the world without having to give up the work in which our Lord decided to call us. Thus, the most important apostolate of Opus Dei is that which each member carries out individually, through his professional work done with the greatest human perfection possible—despite my personal shortcomings and those which each individual may have—in all environments and in all countries: for among the members of Opus Dei there are people of some seventy countries of all races and social conditions.

Besides, Opus Dei as a corporation, with the help of very many people who do not belong to the Work and who often are not Christian, fosters corporate activities through which it seeks to contribute toward solving the many problems which face the world today: educational institutions, welfare centers, schools for professional development and advancement, and so forth.

The university-level institutions of which you speak are another aspect of this task. Their principal features can be summed up as follows: to train people in personal freedom and in personal responsibility. With freedom and responsibility, people work enthusiastically and wholeheartedly, and there is no need for controls or supervision. Everyone feels at home and therefore all you need is a simple schedule. Another characteristic is the spirit of living together in harmony without discrimination of any kind. Here, in this living together, personality takes shape. Each individual learns that in order to be able to demand respect for his own freedom he must respect the freedom of others. Finally, there is the spirit of human brotherhood. Each person's individual talents have to be put to the service of others; if not, they are of little use. The corporate works which Opus Dei runs throughout the world are always at the service of everyone, because they are a Christian service.

In May, when you were with the students of the University of Navarre, you promised a book about student and university matters. Could you tell us whether it will be long in appearing?

Allow an old man over sixty this little vanity. I trust that the book will be published and that it will help teachers and students. At least I will put into it all the love which I have never lost since I first set foot in the university, so many years ago!

It may take a little while yet, but it will come. On another occasion I promised the students of Navarre a statue of the

85

Virgin Mary to put on the campus where she could bless the pure, healthy love of your youth. The statue was some time in coming, but it arrived at last: Holy Mary, Mother of Fair Love, blessed for you especially by the Pope.

As for the book, by the way, you should not expect it to please everyone. I will state my own opinions, which I trust will be respected by those who think the opposite, as I respect all opinions which differ from mine, and as I respect those who have a large and generous heart even though they do not share with me the Christian faith. Let me tell you something that has happened to me often. The last occasion was here in Pamplona. A student came up to me. He wanted to greet me: "Monsignor, I'm not a Christian," he said, "I'm a Moslem."

"You are a son of God, as I am," I answered him. And I embraced him with all my heart.

Finally, could you say something to those of us who work in university journalism?

86   Journalism is a great thing, and so is university journalism. You can contribute a good deal to promote among your fellow students love for noble ideals and a desire to overcome personal egoisms. You can foster an awareness of social problems, you can encourage fraternity. And let me especially invite you to love the truth.

I cannot hide from you that I am disgusted by the sensationalism of some journalists who write half-truths. To inform the public is not to steer a middle course between truth and falsehood. That is not objective information, nor is it moral. People who mix in, together with a few half-truths, a considerable number of errors and even premeditated slanders are unworthy of the name of journalists. They cannot be called journalists because they are only the more or less well-greased tools of any organization for propagating falsehood which knows that lies once put into circulation will be repeated *ad nauseum*, without bad faith, through the ignorance and credulity of many people. I must confess that as far as I am concerned false journalists come out winners, because not a day passes in which I don't pray earnestly for them, asking our Lord to enlighten their consciences.

I ask you, then, to spread the love of good journalism, journalism which is not satisfied with unfounded rumor, with the invention of some overheated imagination which is passed on to the public as "People say that . . ." Report with facts, with results, without judging intentions, upholding the legitimate diversity of opinions in a calm way, without resorting to personal attacks. It is difficult for people to live together harmoniously when there is no real information. And real information does not fear the truth and does not allow itself to be led away by motives of intrigue, false prestige, or economic advantage.

Women in Social Life and in Church Life

Interview with Pilar Salcedo (*Telva*)

Monsignor, the presence of women in social life is extending far beyond the sphere of the family, in which they have moved almost exclusively up to now. What do you think about this development? What, in your opinion, are the main characteristics that women have to develop if they are to fulfill their mission?

87 First let me say that I don't think there need be any conflict between one's family life and social life. Just as in a man's life, but with particular shades of difference, the home and the family will always occupy a central place in the life of a woman. For it is obvious that when she spends time on her family she is fulfilling a great human and Christian role. Nevertheless, this does not exclude the possibility of her having other professional work—for housework is also professional work—in any worthwhile employment available in the society in which she lives. I can understand why you state the problem the way you do. But I think if we systematically contrast work in the home with outside work, retaining the old dichotomy which was formally used to maintain that a woman's place was in the home but switching the stress, it could easily lead, from the social point of view, to a greater mistake than that which we are trying to correct because it would be more serious if it led women to give up their work in the home.

Even on the personal level one cannot flatly affirm that a

woman has to achieve her perfection only outside the home, as if time spent on her family were time stolen from the development of her personality. The home—whatever its characteristics, because a single woman should also have a home—is a particularly suitable place for the growth of her personality. The attention she gives to her family will always be a woman's greatest dignity. In the care she takes of her husband and children or, to put it in more general terms, in her work of creating a warm and formative atmosphere around her, a woman fulfills the most indispensable part of her mission. And so it follows that she can achieve her personal perfection there.

What I have just said does not go against her participating in other aspects of social life, including politics. In these spheres, too, women can offer a valuable personal contribution, without neglecting their special feminine qualities. They will do this to the extent in which they are humanly and professionally equipped. Both family and society clearly need this special contribution, which is in no way secondary to that of men.

Development, maturity, emancipation of women should not mean a pretension to equality, to uniformity with men, a servile *imitation* of a man's way of doing things. That would not get us anywhere. Women would turn out losers, not because they are better than men, or worse, but because they are different.

In terms of fundamentals, one can in fact speak of equal rights which should be legally recognized, both in civil and ecclesiastical law. Women, like men, possess the dignity of being persons and children of God. Nevertheless, on this basis of fundamental equality, each must achieve what is proper to him or her. In this sense a woman's emancipation means that she should have a real possibility of developing her own potentialities to the fullest extent—those which she has personally and those which she has in common with other women. Equal rights and equal opportunities before the law do not suppress this diversity, which enriches all mankind. They presuppose and encourage it.

Women are called to bring to the family, to society and to the Church, characteristics which are their own and which they alone can give: their gentle warmth and untiring generosity, their love for detail, their quick-wittedness and intuition, their simple and deep piety, their constancy.... A woman's femininity is genuine only if she is aware of the beauty of this contribution for which there is no substitute—and if she incorporates it into her own life.

To fulfill this mission, a woman has to develop her own personality and not let herself be carried away by a naïve desire to imitate which, as a rule, would tend to put her in an inferior position and leave her unique qualities unfulfilled. If she is a mature person, with a character and mind of her own, she will indeed accomplish the mission to which she feels called, whatever it may be. Her life and work will be really constructive, fruitful, and full of meaning, whether she spends the day dedicated to her husband and children or whether, having given up the idea of marriage for a noble reason, she has given herself fully to other tasks.

Each woman in her own sphere of life, if she is faithful to her divine and human vocation, can and, in fact, does achieve the fullness of her feminine personality. Let us remember that Mary, Mother of God and Mother of men, is not only a model but also a proof of the transcendental value of an apparently unimportant life.

At times, however, a woman isn't sure of having found the place which suits her and to which she is called. Often if she has a job outside, the demands of the home weigh her down; and if she spends all her time with her family, she feels that her scope is being limited. What would you say to women who have this experience?

This very real feeling is frequently due to particular limitations which we all have because we are human: it comes because we lack well-determined ideals capable of guiding our whole life, or because of a subconscious pride. At times, we would like to be outstanding in everything. And since this is impossible, it leads to confusion and anxiety or even depression and boredom: you cannot do ten things at the same time, you don't know which to do, and you end up doing nothing well. In this situation, jealousy can develop, one's imagination easily becomes escapist and seeks refuge in fantasy which, leaving reality far behind, ends up by weakening one's willpower. It is what I have repeatedly called "mystical wishful thinking," made up of useless daydreams and empty ideals: If only I hadn't married, if only I did not have this job, if only I had better health, or was younger, or had more time!

88

Like everything valuable the solution is costly. It lies in the search for the true center of human life, which can give priority, order, and meaning to everything. We find this center in our relations with God by means of a genuine interior life. By making Christ the center of our lives, we discover the meaning of the mission he has entrusted to us. We have a human ideal that becomes divine. New horizons of hope open up in our life, and we come to the point of sacrificing willingly, not just this or that aspect of our activity, but our whole life, thus giving it, paradoxically, its deepest fulfillment.

The problem you pose is not confined to women. At some time or other, many men experience the same sort of thing, with slightly different characteristics. The source of the trouble is usually the same—lack of a high ideal that can only be discovered with God's light.

But smaller remedies, which *seem* trivial, must also be used. When there are lots of things to do you have to establish priorities, to get organized. Many difficulties stem from downright disorder. There are women who do hundreds of things—and all of them well—because they are well organized and have courageously imposed order on all their work. They know how to concentrate at each moment on what they have to do without getting worried about what's round the corner, or what they might have been able to do before. Others are overwhelmed by all there is to do; and because they are overwhelmed, they don't do anything.

Certainly there will always be many women whose only task is to run their home. This is a wonderful job which is very worthwhile. Through this profession—because it is a profession, in a true and noble sense—they are an influence for good, not only in their family but also among their many friends and acquaintances, among people with whom they come in contact in one way or another. Sometimes their impact is much greater than that of other professional people, to say nothing of when they put their experience and knowledge at the service of hundreds of people in centers devoted to the formation and education of women, like those which my daughters in Opus Dei direct all over the world. Then they teach others to run a home and become educators who are more effective, I would say, than many university professors.

Please excuse me for insisting on the same subject. Through the letters which reach our editor's desk, we know that some mothers of large families complain about their being limited to the role of having children, and they feel dissatisfied about not being able to devote their life to other fields: professional work, cultural activities, social work. . . . What advice would you give them?

Now just a moment! What is social work, if not giving oneself to others, with a sense of dedication and service and contributing effectively to the good of all? The job of a woman in her house is a social contribution in itself, and can easily be the most effective of all.

Take the case of a large family. The mother's work is comparable to that of professional teachers and in many cases leaves them in the shade. A teacher manages to educate a number of boys and girls more or less successfully in the course of his life. A mother can give her children a solid set of values and shape their character and can make them, in their turn, other teachers, thus setting up an uninterrupted chain of responsibility and virtue.

In these matters it is easy to be misled by mere numbers and think that the work of a teacher, who sees hundreds of people pass through his classes, or that of a writer, who reaches thousands of readers, is more valuable. That is all very well, but how many people are really formed by that teacher or writer? A mother has three, five, ten or more children in her care, and she can make of them a true work of art, a marvel of education, of balance and understanding, a model of the Christian way of life. She can teach them to be happy and to make themselves really useful to those around them.

Besides, it is natural for the children to help with the household chores; and a mother who knows how to bring up her children well can manage this. This way she will have spare time which, if used well, will enable her to cultivate her personal interests and talents and enrich her culture. Fortunately, these days there is plenty of technical equipment, household appliances and that sort of thing, which can be great timesavers if they are taken full advantage of and used correctly. As in every field, personal qualities are what count. Some women with the latest-model washing machine take longer to do the washing (and do it worse) than when they did it by hand. Appliances are useful only when one knows how to use them.

I know of many married women with large families who run their homes very well and still find time to cooperate in other apostolic tasks, just like that early Christian married couple, Aquila and Priscilla. They worked in their house and at their job and besides this were splendid cooperators of Saint Paul. With their word and example they brought Apollo to the faith of Jesus Christ, a man who was later to become a great preacher of the early Church. As I have already said, someone who really wants to can overcome quite a number of limitations, without neglecting any of his duties. In fact, there is time for a lot of things: for running a home with professional outlook, for giving oneself continually to others, for improving one's own culture and enriching that of others, and for carrying out many other effective tasks.

You refer to the presence of women in public life, in politics. What do you consider the specific task of women in this field?

90   The presence of women in the whole range of social life is a logical and entirely positive phenomenon, part of the broader phenomenon which I referred to earlier. A modern democratic society has to recognize women's right to take an active part in political life and has to create conditions favorable for everyone who wants to exercise this right.

A woman who wants to play an active role in public affairs has an obligation to prepare herself adequately, so that the part she takes in the life of the community can be responsible and positive. All professional work demands previous training and a constant effort to improve one's training and adapt it to the new circumstances that may arise. And this is very specially true for those who aspire to occupy leading positions in society, because they are called to a very important service on which the entire community's well-being depends.

A woman with adequate training should find the field of public life open to her at all levels. In this sense it is impossible to point out specific tasks that correspond to women alone. As I said earlier, in this field what is specific is not the task or position in itself, but the way in which the work is done. There are values which a woman more readily perceives, and her specific contribution will often, therefore, change the whole approach to a problem and can lead to the discovery of completely new approaches.

By virtue of their special gifts, women can greatly enrich civil life. This is very obvious, for example, in the sphere of family or social legislation. Feminine qualities offer the best guarantee that genuine human and Christian values will be respected when it comes to taking measures that affect family life, education, and the future of youth.

I have just mentioned the importance of Christian values in the solution of social and family problems, and I want to stress their particular importance in all public life. Just as for a man, when a woman takes part in political activity her Christian faith confers on her the responsibility of carrying out a genuine apostolate, that is to say, a Christian service to the whole of society. This does not mean representing the Church officially or semi-officially in public life, and even less using the Church for one's own personal career of for party interests. On the contrary, it means forming your own opinions with freedom in all those temporal matters in which Christians are free, and accepting personal responsibility for your opinions and actions, which should be always in keeping with the faith you profess.

In the homily you gave in Pamplona last October during the Mass you celebrated at the assembly of the Friends of the University of Navarre (see chapter 8), you spoke of human love in words which made a deep impression on us. Many readers have written commenting on the impact they felt on hearing you. What would you say are the most important values of Christian marriage?

91   The majority of the members of Opus Dei are married people, so in this field I can speak from the experience of many years of priestly activity in many countries. For the married members of Opus Dei human love and marriage duties are part of their divine vocation. Opus Dei has made of marriage a divine way, a vocation, and this has many consequences for personal holiness and for apostolate. I have spent almost forty years preaching the vocational meaning of marriage. More than once I have had occasion to see faces light up, as men and women who had thought that in their lives a dedication to God was incompatible with a noble and pure human love heard me say that marriage is a divine path on earth!

The purpose of marriage is to help married people sanctify themselves and others. For this reason they receive a special grace in the sacrament instituted by Jesus Christ. Those who are called to the married state will, with the grace of God, find within their state everything they need to be holy, to identity themselves each day more with Jesus Christ, and to lead those with whom they live to God.

That is why I always look with hope and affection upon Christian homes, upon all the families which are the fruit of the sacrament of matrimony. They are a shining witness of the great divine mystery of Christ's loving union with his Church which Saint Paul calls *sacramentum magnum*, a great sacrament (Eph 5: 32). We must strive so that these cells of Christianity may be born and may develop with a desire for holiness, conscious of the fact that the sacrament of initiation—Baptism—confers on all Christians a divine mission that each must fulfill in his own walk of life.

Christian couples should be aware that they are called to sanctity themselves and to sanctify others, that they are called to be apostles, and that their first apostolate is in the home. They should understand that founding a family, educating their children, and exercising a Christian influence in society are a supernatural task. The effectiveness and the success of their life—their happiness—depends to a great extent on their awareness of their specific mission.

But they mustn't forget that the secret of married happiness lies in everyday things, not in daydreams. It lies in finding the hidden joy of coming home in the evening; in affectionate relations with their children; in everyday work in which the whole family cooperates; in good humor in the face of difficulties that should be met with a sporting spirit; in making the best use of all the advances that civilization offers to help us bring up children, to make the house pleasant, and life more simple.

I continually tell those who have been called by God to form a home to love one another always, to love each other with the love of their youth. Anyone who thinks that love ends when the worries and difficulties that life brings with it begin, has a poor idea of marriage, which is a sacrament and an ideal and a vocation. It is precisely then that love grows strong. Torrents of worries and difficulties are incapable of drowning true love because people who sacrifice themselves generously together are brought closer by their sacrifice. As Scripture says, *aquae multae*—a host of difficulties, physical and moral—*non potuerunt extinguere caritatem*—cannot extinguish love (Song 8: 7).

We know that the idea of marriage as a way of holiness is not new in your preaching. As far back as 1934, when you wrote Consideraciones Espirituales, *you insisted on the fact that marriage should be seen as a vocation. But in this book and, later, in* The Way, *you also wrote that marriage is for "the soldiers" and not for "the General Staff of Christ's army." Could you explain how these two points can be reconciled?*

92 In the spirit and life of Opus Dei there has never been any difficulty in reconciling them. To begin with, it is well to remember that the greater excellence of celibacy, chosen for spiritual motives, is not a theological opinion of mine but part of the Church's faith.

When I wrote those words back in the thirties, there was a tendency among Catholics, particularly in the spheres of day-to-day pastoral activity, to encourage the search for Christian perfection among young people only by making them appreciate the supernatural value of virginity, while neglecting to mention the value of marriage as a way of holiness.

In general, schools did not teach young people to see the true dignity of marriage. Even now it is quite common, in the retreats given to pupils during their last year at secondary school, to stress subjects related to a possible religious vocation rather than to a possible vocation to marriage. There are still some people, though they are gradually disappearing, who undervalue married life, giving young people the impression that it is something the Church simply tolerates, as if marriage precluded any serious striving for sanctity.

In Opus Dei we have always acted differently. While making clear the purpose and the excellence of apostolic celibacy, we have pointed out that marriage is a divine way on earth.

I am not afraid of human love—that holy love of my parents which our Lord used to give me life. I bless this love with both hands. The partners are both the ministers and the matter of the sacrament of marriage, as the bread and wine are the matter of the sacrament of the holy Eucharist. That's why I like all the songs about pure human love; for in them I find, interwoven, both human and divine love. But, also, I always say that people who follow a vocation to apostolic celibacy are not old maids who do not understand or value love; on the contrary, their lives can only be explained in terms of this divine Love (I like to write it with a capital letter) which is the very essence of every Christian vocation.

There is nothing contradictory about being fully aware of the value of the vocation to marriage and understanding the greater excellence of the vocation to celibacy *propter regnum caelorum*—for love of the kingdom of heaven (Mt 19:12). I am convinced that any Christian who tries to know, accept, and love the teaching of the Church will understand perfectly how the two are compatible if he tries also to know, accept, and love his own personal vocation. That is to say, if he has faith and lives by it.

When I wrote that marriage is for the "soldiers," I only described what has happened always in the Church. As you know, the bishops—who form the Episcopal College, which has the Pope as its head, and who govern with him the entire Church—are elected from among those who live celibacy. The same is true in the Eastern Church, in which there are married priests. Furthermore, it can be easily understood and shown that those who are celibate are *de facto* freer of ties of affection and have greater freedom of movement to dedicate themselves permanently to running and supporting apostolic undertakings; this is also true in the lay apostolate. This does not mean to say that the rest of the laity cannot, or do not in fact, carry out a splendid apostolate and one of prime importance. It only means that there are different duties, different forms of dedication in positions of diverse responsibility.

In an army—and this is all the comparison was meant to express—the soldiers are as necessary as the general staff and can be more heroic and merit more glory. In a word, there is a variety of tasks, and all are necessary and worthy. What is really important is that each person should follow his own vocation. For each individual, the most perfect thing is, always and only, to do God's will.

And so a Christian who seeks to sanctify himself in the married state and is conscious of the greatness of his own vocation spontaneously feels a special veneration and deep affection toward those who are called to apostolic celibacy. When one of his children, by God's grace, sets out on this path, he truly rejoices and comes to love his own vocation to marriage even more because it has permitted him to offer the fruits of human love to Jesus Christ, who is the great Love of all men, married or celibate.

Many married couples find themselves confused regarding the number of children they should have by the advice they receive—at times from some priests. What advice would you give them?

93   Those who confuse people's consciences in this way forget that life is sacred. They deserve the severe reproaches that our Lord made to the blind who lead the blind, to those who do not want to enter the kingdom of heaven and do not let others enter either. I do not judge their intentions, and in fact I am sure that many give such advice guided by compassion and a desire to find a solution to difficult situations. I cannot, however, hide the fact that I am deeply saddened by the destructive and in many cases devilish work of those who not only fail to give sound doctrine but go further and undermine the teaching of the Church.

Married couples should remember, when they receive advice and recommendations on this matter, that what they have to do is to discover what God wants of them. With sincerity, a right intention, and a minimum of Christian formation, our conscience knows how to discover God's will in this sphere as in others. There are cases in which we seek advice that will favor our own selfishness, and suppress with its apparent authority the voice of our inner convictions. Then we even go from adviser to adviser until we find a "benevolent" one. This is a pharisaical attitude which is unworthy of a child of God.

The advice of another Christian and especially a priest's advice, in questions of faith or morals, is a powerful help for knowing what God wants of us in our particular circumstances. Advice, however, does not eliminate personal responsibility. In the end, it is we ourselves, each one of us on our own, who have to decide for ourselves and personally account to God for our decisions.

Over and above any private advice stands God's law, which is contained in Sacred Scripture, guarded and taught by the Magisterium of the Church with the assistance of the Holy Spirit. When a particular piece of advice contradicts God's word as taught by the Magisterium, we have to reject it decisively. God will give his grace to those who act with an upright intention. He will inspire them as to what to do, and, when necessary, he will enable them to find a priest who knows how to lead their souls along pure and right paths even though at times they may be difficult ones.

Spiritual guidance should not be used to turn people into beings with no judgment of their own, who limit themselves to carrying out mechanically what others tell them. On the contrary, it should tend to develop men with their own Christian standards. This requires maturity, firm convictions, sufficient doctrinal knowledge, a refined spirit, and an educated will.

It is important for married people to acquire a clear sense of the dignity of their vocation. They must know that they have been called by God not only to human love but also to a divine love, through their human love. It is important for them to realize that they have been chosen from eternity to cooperate with the creative power of God by having and then bringing up children. Our Lord asks them to make their home and their entire family life a testimony of all the Christian virtues.

I shall never tire of repeating that marriage is a great and marvelous divine path. Like everything divine in us, it calls for response to grace, generosity, dedication, and service. Selfishness, in whatever shape or form, is opposed to the love of God, which ought to govern our lives. This is a fundamental point which one must always bear in mind with regard to marriage and the number of children.

There are some women who have had many children already and are afraid to tell their friends and relations that they are going to have another child. They fear the criticism of those who think that, now "the pill" has arrived, large families are old-fashioned. Indeed, it can be difficult to bring up a large family in contemporary society. What would you say to us on the subject?

94   I bless parents who, joyfully accepting the mission that God entrusts to them, have many children. Moreover, I ask married couples not to block the wellsprings of life, and I invite them to have enough supernatural outlook and courage to bring up a large family, if it is God's will.

When I praise large families, I do not refer to those which are the result of mere physiological relations. I refer to families founded on the practice of human virtues which have a high regard for personal dignity and know that giving children to God consists not only in engendering their natural life but also undertaking the lengthy task of their upbringing. Giving of life comes first, but it is not everything.

There may be particular cases in which God's will, which shows itself in ordinary ways, is precisely that a family be small. Nevertheless, the theories that make birth control an ideal, or a universal or general duty, are criminal, anti-Christian, and humanly degrading. To appeal to a presumed post-conciliar spirit opposed to large families would be to adulterate and pervert Christian doctrine. The Second Vatican Council has proclaimed that "especially worthy of mention among the married people who fulfill the mission entrusted to them by God are those who, with prudent mutual agreement, generously accept a more numerous offspring to educate worthily" (Constitution *Gaudium et spes*, no. 50). Moreover, Pope Paul VI, in an address of February 12, 1966, commented "that the recently concluded Second Vatican Council should diffuse among Christian couples a spirit of generosity in order to increase the new People of God . . . that they should always remember that this expansion of God's kingdom and the possibilities of the Church's penetration among mankind in order to bring about eternal salvation and the salvation of the world are also entrusted to their generosity."

The number is not in itself the decisive factor. The fact of having few or many children does not on its own make a family more or less Christian. What matters is the integrity and honesty with which married life is lived. True mutual love transcends the union of husband and wife and extends to its natural fruits—the children. Selfishness, on the contrary, sooner or later reduces love to a mere satisfaction of instinct and destroys the bond which unites parents and children. A child who suspects that he has come into the world against his parents' will, who feels he was born not of a pure love but because of miscalculation or oversight, can hardly consider himself a good son—a true son—of his parents.

I was saying that, in itself, the number of children is not a decisive factor. Nevertheless, I see clearly that attacks on large families stem from a lack of faith. They are the product of a social atmosphere which is incapable of understanding generosity, trying to conceal selfishness and unmentionable practices under apparently altruistic motives. Paradoxically, the countries where most birth control propaganda is found, and which impose birth control on other countries, are precisely the ones which have attained a higher standard of living. Perhaps their economic and social arguments in favor of birth control could be taken more seriously if they led them to give away a sizable part of their great wealth to those in need. Until then it will be hard not to think that the real motive behind their arguments is hedonism and ambition for political domination, for demographic neo-colonialism.

I am not unaware of the great problems facing humanity, nor of the concrete difficulties which a particular family can come up against. I often think of this and my fatherly heart, which I have to have as a Christian and as a priest, is filled with compassion. Nevertheless, it is not lawful to look for the solution in this direction.

95   I do not understand how Catholics and even priests have for years advised, with an easy conscience, the use of the pill to prevent conception. The teachings of the popes cannot be disregarded just like that. Nor ought they to allege, as they do with incredible flippancy, that the Pope when he does not speak *ex cathedra* is simply a private theologian subject to error. To say nothing of the tremendous arrogance, it supposes to affirm that the Pope makes mistakes while they do not.

Besides, they forget that the Pope is not only a teacher, and infallible when he says so expressly, but also the chief legislator. In this case Pope Paul VI has laid down in un-equivocal terms that all the dispositions of the much revered Pius XII in this very delicate matter are still binding and must necessarily be followed. Moreover, Pius XII only permitted some natural procedures—not the pill—to avoid conception in isolated and difficult cases. To advise the contrary is, there-fore, a serious act of disobedience to the Holy Father in a grave matter.

I could write a huge volume on the disastrous conse-quences that the use of these and other contraceptives brings with it, namely: the breakdown of married love (the married couple come to see each other as accomplices rather than as husband and wife), unhappiness, infidelity, mental and spiri-tual distress, great harm to the children, a loss of married peace. . . . However, I don't think it is necessary to go into all this; I prefer simply to obey the Pope. If, at some time, he were to decide that the use of a particular medicine were licit to prevent conception, I should adapt myself to whatever he said. And, following the norms established by the Pope and those of moral theology, I would examine in each case the evident dangers to which I have just referred and would give my advice in conscience to each individual.

And I would always bear in mind that our present-day world will not be saved by men who aim to drug the spiritual life and reduce everything to a question of economics or material well-being. Its salvation will come from men and women who know that moral law is geared to man's eternal destiny, who have faith in God and generously face up to the demands of their faith, helping those around them to appreci-ate the transcendental meaning of our life on earth.

This certainty should lead them not to encourage escap-ism but to ensure effectively that all men have the necessary material resources, that there be work for all, and that no one find himself unjustly confined in his social and family life.

The frustration caused by not being able to have children leads at times to discord and misunderstanding. In your opinion, what meaning should Christian couples who are childless give to their married life?

96   In the first place I would tell them that they should not give up hope too easily. They should ask God to give them children and, if it is his will, to bless them as he blessed the Patriarchs of the Old Testament. And then it would be good for both of them to see a good doctor. If in spite of everything God does not give them children, they should not regard themselves as being thwarted. They should be happy, discovering in this very fact God's will for them. Often God does not give children because he is asking more. God asks them to put the same effort and the same kind and gentle dedication into helping their neighbors as they would have put into raising their children, without the human joy that comes from having children. There is, then, no reason for feeling they are failures or for giving way to sadness.

If the married couple have interior life, they will understand that God is urging them to make their lives a generous Christian service, a different apostolate from the one they would have fulfilled with their children, but an equally marvelous one.

If they look around they will discover people who need help, charity, and love. There are, moreover, many apostolic tasks in which they can work. If they give themselves generously to others and forget themselves, if they put their hearts into their work, they will be wonderfully fruitful and will experience a spiritual parenthood that will fill their souls with true peace.

The particular way of doing this may vary in each case, but in the last analysis it is a matter of being concerned for others with a sense of loving service. God, who always rewards, will fill with a deep joy those souls who have had the generous humility of not thinking of themselves.

There are marriages in which the wife, for some reason or other, finds herself separated from her husband in degrading and unbearable conditions. In these cases it is difficult for her to accept the indissolubility of the marriage bond. Women in these circumstances complain that they are denied the possibility of building a new home. What answer would you give to people in such a situation?

While understanding their suffering, I would tell them that   97 they can also see in their situation God's will, which is never cruel, for God is a loving Father. The situation may be especially difficult for some time, but if they go to our Lord and his blessed Mother they will receive the help of grace.

The indissolubility of marriage is not a caprice of the Church, nor is it merely a positive ecclesiastical law. It is a precept of natural law, of divine law, and responds perfectly to our nature and to the supernatural order of grace. For these reasons, in the great majority of cases, indissolubility is an indispensable condition for the happiness of married couples and for the spiritual security of their children. Even in the very sad cases we are talking about, the humble acceptance of God's will always brings with it a profound sense of satisfaction that nothing can substitute. It is not merely a refuge, or a consolation: it is the very essence of Christian life.

If women who are separated from their husbands have children in their care, they should understand that their children continue to need their loving motherly devotion, and especially now, to make up for the deficiencies of a divided home. They should make a generous effort to understand that indissolubility, which for them means sacrifice, is a safeguard for the integrity and unity of the great majority of families and ennobles the parent's love and prevents the abandonment of the children.

Surprise at the apparent hardness of the Christian precept of indissolubility is nothing new. The Apostles were surprised when Jesus confirmed it. It can seem a burden, a yoke, but Christ himself said that his yoke was sweet and his burden light.

On the other hand, although recognizing the inevitable hardship of a good many situations, which often could and should have been avoided, we should be careful not to over-dramatize. Is the life of a woman in these circumstances really harder than that of other maltreated women or of people who suffer any of the other great physical or moral sorrows that life brings with it?

What really makes a person unhappy and even destroys a whole society is the frenzied search of well-being and the attempt to eliminate at all costs all difficulties and hardships. Life has many facets, very different situations. Some are harsh, others may seem easy. Each situation brings its own grace. Each one is a special call from God, a new opportunity to work and to give the divine testimony of charity. I would advise those who feel oppressed by a difficult situation to try to forget about their own problems a bit and concern themselves with the problems of others. If they do this they will have more peace, and, above all, they will sanctify themselves.

One of the great blessings a family can enjoy is the peace of a stable family life. Unfortunately, however, quite a few families are divided over political or social questions. How do you think these conflicts can be overcome?

98   I have only one prescription: strive to live together in harmony and to understand and pardon each other. The fact that someone thinks differently from me (especially in matters

which are open to personal opinion) in no way justifies an attitude of personal enmity, nor even of coldness or indifference. My Christian faith tells me to have charity for everyone, including those who do not have the grace of believing in Jesus Christ. Just think, then, how much greater must be the obligation to have charity when people are united by the same blood and the same faith and divided only by differences of opinion. Besides, since in these matters no one can claim to be in possession of absolute truth, friendly and loving relations offer a real opportunity for learning from others what they can teach us. All the members of the family can learn something from the others if they want to.

It is not Christian, or even human, for a family to be divided over such matters. When the value of freedom is fully understood and the divine gift of freedom is passionately loved, the pluralism that freedom brings with it is also loved.

I will tell you what happens in Opus Dei, which is a large family where all are united by the same spiritual aims. In everything that is not a matter of faith, each member thinks and acts as he wishes with complete freedom and personal responsibility. The pluralism which, logically and sociologically, derives from this fact does not create any problems for the Work. Rather, it is a sign of good spirit. Precisely because pluralism is not feared in Opus Dei but loved as a legitimate consequence of personal freedom, the different opinions of the members in Opus Dei are no obstacle to charity and mutual understanding in their dealings with each other. Freedom and charity—I always come back to them because, in fact, they are essential conditions. We must live with the freedom Christ won for us and with the charity he gave us as a new commandment.

You have just spoken about family unity as a great value. In view of this fact, how is it that Opus Dei does not organize activities of spiritual formation for husbands and wives together?

99   In this, as in so many other aspects of life, Christians can choose different solutions in accordance with their own preferences or opinions, and no one may impose an exclusive system upon them. We should flee like the plague from that approach to pastoral work and the apostolate in general which seems to be no more than a revised and enlarged edition, in religious life, of the one-party system. I know that there are Catholic groups that organize retreats and other formative activities for married couples. I have no objection whatever to their doing what they think best nor to people taking part in their activities if they find that they help them live their Christian vocation better. But I do not consider this the only way of doing things, and it is by no means self-evident that it is the best.

There are many facets of Christian life in which married couples, and, in fact, the whole family can and at times should take part together, such as the Eucharistic sacrifice and other acts of worship. I think, nevertheless, that certain activities of spiritual formation are more effective if they are attended separately by husband and wife. For one thing, it highlights the fundamentally personal character of one's own sanctification, of the ascetic struggle, of union with God. These certainly affect others, but the role of the individual conscience in them is vital and cannot be substituted. Furthermore, it makes it easier to suit the formation given to the particular needs, circumstances, and psychology of each person. This does not mean to say that in these activities the fact that the participants are married is disregarded; nothing could be further removed from the spirit of Opus Dei.

For forty years I have been preaching and writing that

each person has to sanctify himself in ordinary life, in the concrete situations of everyday. Married people, therefore, have to sanctify themselves by living their family obligations perfectly. One of the aims of the retreats and other means of formation organized by Opus Dei for married men or women is to make them more fully aware of the dignity of their vocation to marriage and help them prepare themselves, with the grace of God, to live it better.

In many aspects the demands which married love makes on men and on women are different, and their love shows itself in different ways. With specific means of formation they can be effectively helped to discover these details of love in their daily lives. In this way, separation for a few hours or a few days will, in the long run, make them more united and help them to love each other more and better than they did before with a love full of respect.

I repeat that we do not claim that our way of acting in this is the only good one, or that it should be adopted by every-one. It simply seems to me that it gives very good results and that there are strong reasons—as well as long experience—for doing things this way, but I do not take issue with the contrary opinion. Furthermore, I should add that if in Opus Dei we adopt this procedure in certain types of spiritual formation, nevertheless, in numerous other activities married couples as such participate and cooperate. I am thinking, for example, of the work which is done with the parents of pupils in schools run by members of Opus Dei: in the meetings, lectures, and the like, especially arranged for the parents of students who live in halls of residence run by the Work.

So you see, when the type of activity requires the presence of the married couple, husband and wife both take part. But these types of meetings and activities are different from those that are directed toward personal spiritual training.

*Still on the subject of the family, I would now like to
turn to the education of the children and the relations
between parents and children. The changes that have
affected family life in recent years sometimes make
mutual understanding difficult and even lead to a breakdown in communication, to what has been called the
"generation gap." How can this be overcome?*

100   The problem is an old one, although perhaps it arises now
more frequently or more acutely because of the rapid evolution that characterizes modern society. It is perfectly understandable and natural that young and older people should see
things differently. This has always been the case. The surprising thing would be if a teenager were to think just as an adult
does. We all felt a tendency to rebel against our elders when
we began to form our own judgment autonomously. But we
have come to understand, with the passing of the years, that
our parents were right in many things in which they were
guided by their experience and their love. That's why it is up
to the parents to make the first move. They have already
passed through this stage. It is up to them to be very understanding, to have flexibility and good humor, avoiding any
possible conflicts simply by being affectionate and farsighted.
I always advise parents to try to be friends with their children. The parental authority which the upbringing of children requires can be perfectly harmonized with friendship,
which means putting themselves in some way on the same
level as their children. Children—even those who seem in-
tractable and unresponsive—always want this closeness, this
fraternity, with their parents. It is a question of trust. Parents
should bring up their children in an atmosphere of friendship, never giving the impression that they do not trust them.
They should give them freedom and teach them how to use it
with personal responsibility. It is better for parents to let

themselves be fooled once in a while, because the trust they have shown will make the children themselves feel ashamed of having abused it—they will correct themselves. On the other hand, if they have no freedom, if they see that no one trusts them, they will always be inclined to deceive their parents.

This friendship, this knowing how to put oneself on the childrens' level, makes it easier for them to talk about their small problems; it also makes it possible for the parents to be the ones who teach them gradually about the origin of life, in accordance with their mentality and capacity to understand, gently anticipating their natural curiosity. I consider this very important. There is no reason why children should associate sex with something sinful or find out about something that is in itself noble and holy in a vulgar conversation with a friend. It can also be an important step in strengthening the friendship between parents and children, preventing a separation in the early moments of their moral life.

Parents should also endeavor to stay young at heart so as to find it easier to react sympathetically toward the noble aspirations and even toward the extravagant fantasies of their youngsters. Life changes, and there are many new things which we may not like. Perhaps objectively speaking they are no better than others that have gone before; but they are not bad. They are simply other ways of living and nothing more. On more than one occasion conflicts may arise because importance is attached to petty differences which could be overcome with a little common sense and good humor.

However, not everything depends on the parents. The children also have to play their part. Young people are always capable of getting enthusiastic about great undertakings, high ideals, and anything that is genuine. They must be helped to understand the simple, natural, and often unappreciated beauty of their parents' lives. Children should come to real-

101

ize, little by little, the sacrifices their parents have made for them, the often heroic self-denial that has gone into raising the family. They should also learn not to overdramatize, not to think themselves misunderstood; nor to forget that they will always be in debt to their parents. And as they will never be able to repay what they owe, their response should be to treat their parents with veneration and grateful, filial love.

Let's be frank—the normal thing is for the family to be united. There may be friction and differences, but that's quite normal. In a certain sense it even adds flavor to our daily life. These problems are insignificant; time always takes care of them. What remains firm is love, a true and sincere love which comes from being generous and brings with it a concern for one another, and which enables the members of the family to sense each other's difficulties and offer tactful solutions. Because this is the normal thing, the vast majority of people understand me perfectly when they hear me say (I have been repeating it since the 1920s) that the fourth commandment of the Decalogue is a "most sweet precept."

Perhaps as a reaction to compulsory religious education, reduced at times to a few routine and external practices, some young people today pay almost no attention to Christian piety because they consider it sentimental nonsense. What solution would you suggest for this problem?

102   The question carries its own answer. The meaning of true piety should be taught first by example and then by word. False piety is a sad pseudo-spiritual caricature which generally results from a lack of doctrine and from a certain psychological defect. The logical result is that it is repellent to anyone who loves authenticity and sincerity.

I am very glad to see how Christian piety takes root among young people today, as it did forty years ago,

— when they see it lived sincerely in the lives of others;

— when they understand that prayer is speaking with God, not anonymously, but personally, as a father and friend, in a heart-to-heart conversation;

— when we try to make them hear deep in their souls the words with which Jesus Christ himself invites them to a confidential encounter: *vos autem dixi amicos* ["I have called you friends"] (Jn 15:15);

— when a strong appeal is made to their faith, so they see that our Lord is the "same yesterday and today and forever" (Heb 13:8).

It is essential for them to realize that simple and heartfelt piety also calls for the exercise of human virtues and that it cannot be reduced to a few daily or weekly pious acts. It has to penetrate our entire life and give meaning to our work, rest, friendships, and entertainment, to everything we do. We are children of God all day long, even though we do set aside special moments for considering it so that we can fill ourselves with the awareness of our divine filiation, which is the essence of true piety.

I was saying that young people understand this very well. I might add that anyone who tries to live it will always feel young. A Christian who lives in union with Jesus Christ can relish, even if he is eighty, the words we pray at the foot of the altar: "I will go unto the altar of God, of God who gives joy to my youth" (Ps 42:4).

Do you consider it important, then, to teach children to practice their faith from their earliest years? Do you think some acts of piety should be lived in the family?

I think it is precisely the best way to give children a truly   103
Christian upbringing. Scripture tells us about those early
Christian families which drew new strength and new life

from the light of the gospel. Saint Paul calls them "the Church in the household" (1 Cor 16:19).

Experience shows in all Christian environments what good effects come from this natural and supernatural introduction to the life of piety given in the warmth of the home. Children learn to place God first and foremost in their affections. They learn to see God as their Father and Mary as their Mother and learn to pray following their parents' example. In this way one can easily see what a wonderful apostolate parents have and how it is their duty to live a fully Christian life of prayer, so they can communicate their love of God to their children, which is something more than just teaching them.

How can they go about this? They have excellent means in the few, short, daily religious practices that have always been lived in Christian families and which I think are marvelous: grace at meals, morning and night prayers, the family rosary (even though nowadays this devotion to our Lady has been criticized by some people). Customs vary from place to place, but I think one should always encourage some acts of piety which the family can do together in a simple and natural fashion.

This is the way to ensure that God is not regarded as a stranger whom we go to see in church once a week on Sunday. He will be seen and treated as he really is, not only in church but also at home, because our Lord has told us, "Where two or three are gathered together in my name, I am there in the midst of them" (Mt 18:20).

I still pray aloud the bedside prayers I learnt as a child from my mother's lips, and I say so with the pride and gratitude of a son. They bring me closer to God and make me feel the love with which I learned to take my first steps as a Christian. And as I offer to God the day that is beginning, or thank him for the day that is drawing to a close, I ask him to increase in heaven the happiness of those whom I especially love and to unite us there forever.

May I ask another question about young people? Many of their problems reach us through our magazine. One of the most common arises when parents seek to impose their ideas on their children, deciding their future for them. This happens both when it is a question of deciding on a career or job and in the choice of a boy- or girl-friend. It is even more frequent if they are thinking of following a call from God to work in the service of souls. Is there any justification for this attitude on the part of parents? Doesn't it violate the freedom which young people need if they are to become personally mature?

In the final analysis, it is clear that the decisions that deter- 104
mine the course of an entire life have to be taken by each individual personally, with freedom, without coercion or pressure of any kind. This is not to say that the intervention of others is not usually necessary. Precisely because they are decisive steps that affect an entire life and because a person's happiness depends to a great extent on the decisions made, it is clear that they should be taken calmly, without precipitation. They should be particularly responsible and prudent decisions. And part of prudence consists precisely in seeking advice. It would be presumption—for which we usually pay dearly—to think that we can decide alone, without the grace of God and without the love and guidance of other people and, especially, of our parents.

Parents can and should be a great help to their children. They can open new horizons for them, share their experiences, and make them reflect, so they do not allow themselves to be carried away by passing emotional experiences. They can offer them a realistic scale of values. Sometimes they can help with personal advice; on other occasions they should encourage their children to seek other suitable people, such as a loyal and sincere friend, a learned and holy priest, or an expert in career guidance.

Advice does not take away freedom. It gives elements on which to judge, and thus enlarges the possibilities of choice and ensures that decisions are not taken on the basis of irrational factors. After bearing the opinions of others and taking everything into consideration, there comes a moment in which a choice has to be made, and then no one has the right to force a young person's freedom. Parents have to be on guard against the temptation of wanting to project themselves unduly in their children or of molding them according to their own preferences. They should respect their individual God-given inclinations and aptitudes. If their love is true, this is easy enough. Even in the extreme case, when a young person makes a decision that his parents have good reason to consider mistaken and when they think it will lead to future unhappiness, the answer lies not in force, but in understanding. Very often it consists in knowing how to stand by him so as to help him overcome the difficulties and, if necessary, draw all the benefit possible from an unfortunate situation.

After giving their advice and suggestions, parents who sincerely love and seek the good of their children should step tactfully into the background so that nothing can stand in the way of the great gift of freedom that makes man capable of loving and serving God. They should remember that God himself has wanted to be loved and served with freedom, and he always respects our personal decisions. Scripture tell us "When God created man, he made him subject to his own free choice" (Sir 15: 14).

Just a few words more to refer in particular to the last case that you mentioned, the decision to give oneself to the service of the Church and of souls. I think Catholic parents who do not understand this type of vocation have failed in their mission of forming a Christian family. They probably are not aware of the dignity that Christianity gives to their vocation to marriage. But my experience in Opus Dei is very positive. I often tell the members of the Work that they owe ninety percent of their vocation to their parents because they have known how to educate their children and have taught them to be generous. I can assure you that in the vast majority of cases, practically in all, the parents respect and love their children's decision. They immediately see the Work as an extension of their own family. It is one of my greatest joys and yet another proof that in order to be very divine you have to be very human as well.

The theory that love justifies everything is current today, and as a result engagement is looked upon by some people as a sort of "trial marriage." They say it is hypocritical and reactionary not to follow what they consider to be imperative demands of love. What do you think of this attitude?

Any decent person and especially a Christian would consider 　105
it an attitude unworthy of men. It debases human love, confusing it with selfishness and pleasure.

Reactionary? Who are the reactionaries? The real reactionaries are the people who go back to the jungle, recognizing no impulse other than instinct. Engagement should be time for growing in affection and for getting to know each other better. As in every school of love, it should be inspired not by a desire to get but by a spirit of giving, of understanding, of respect and gentle consideration. Just over a year ago, with this in mind, I gave the University of Navarre a statue of the Virgin Mary, Mother of Fair Love, so that the undergraduates who study there might learn from her the nobility of love, human love included.

A trial marriage? How little anyone who uses the term knows of love! Love is a much surer, more real, more human reality. It cannot be treated as a commercial product that is tested and then accepted or rejected on the basis of whim, comfort, and interest.

This lack of moral standards is so pitiful that it does not even seem necessary to condemn people who think or act in this way. They condemn themselves to the barrenness, the sadness, the desolate loneliness they will suffer within a very few years. I never stop praying for them, loving them with all my heart and trying to make them understand that the way back to Christ is always open. They can be saints, upright Christians, if they make an effort. They will lack neither the necessary grace nor our Lord's pardon. Only then will they really understand love—divine Love and also noble human love. And only then will they experience peace, happiness, and fruitfulness.

One great problem of society is that of single women.
We refer particularly to those who had a vocation to
marriage and did not marry. As a result they ask, "What
is our purpose in the world?" What reply would you give
them?

106   "What is our purpose in the world?" To love God with all our heart and all our souls and to spread this love to all. Does that seem little? God does not abandon any soul to a blind destiny. He has a plan for all, and he calls each to a very personal and non-transferable vocation.

Matrimony is a divine way and a vocation, but it is not the only way nor the only vocation. God's plans for each particular woman do not necessarily involve marriage.

You say they had a vocation to marriage and did not manage to find a husband. In some cases that may be true. And at times self-love or egoism may have kept God's call from being fulfilled. In most cases, however, it may be a sign that our Lord has not really given them a vocation to marriage. I admit they like children; they feel they would make good mothers and would give themselves wholeheartedly and faithfully to their children and their husband. However, this is normal in every woman, including those who because of a divine vocation give up the possibility of marriage in order to work in the service of God and souls.

They have not married. Very well then, let them go on loving the will of our Lord as they have up to now, keeping close to his most loving heart. Jesus never abandons us; he is always faithful. He takes care of us in every moment of our lives, giving himself to us now and forever.

Moreover, a woman can fulfill her mission as a woman (with all her feminine characteristics, including her maternal sentiments) in environments outside her own family. For example, in other families, in a school, in social work. The possibilities are endless. Society is at times very hard, and unjustly so, on those it calls "old maids." There are single women who are a source of happiness and peace. They see that things get done and spend themselves generously in the service of others. They are mothers in a deeper and more real way than many who are mothers only in a physiological sense.

My previous questions have referred to engagement. Turning to the topic of marriage, what would you advise married women to do to ensure their marriages continue to be happy with the passing of the years and do not give way to monotony? This question may not seem very important, but we receive many letters on this subject.

107   I think it is in fact an important question, and therefore the possible solutions are also important even though they may seem very obvious. If a marriage is to preserve its initial charm and beauty, both husband and wife should try to renew their love day after day, and that is done through sacrifice, with smiles and also with ingenuity. Is it surprising that a husband who arrives home tired from work begins to lose patience when his wife keeps on and on about everything she thinks has gone wrong during the day? Disagreeable things can wait for a better moment when the husband is less tired and more disposed to listen to them.

Another important thing is personal appearance. And I would say that any priest who says the contrary is a bad adviser. As years go by a woman who lives in the world has to take more care not only of her interior life but also of her looks. Her interior life itself requires her to be careful about her personal appearance; naturally this should always be in keeping with her age and circumstances. I often say jokingly that older façades need more restoration. It is the advice of a priest. An old Spanish saying goes: "A well-groomed woman keeps her husband away from other doors."

That's why I am not afraid to say that women are responsible for eighty percent of the infidelities of their husbands because they do not know how to win them each day and take loving and considerate care of them. A married woman's attention should be centered on her husband and children as a married man's should be centered on his wife and children. Much time and effort is required to succeed in this, and anything which militates against it is bad and shouldn't be tolerated.

There is no excuse for not fulfilling this lovable duty. Work outside the home is not an excuse. Not even one's life of piety can be an excuse, because if it is incompatible with one's daily obligations it is not good or pleasing to God. A married woman's first concern has to be her home. There is an Aragonese saying which goes: "If through going to church to pray a woman burns her stew, she may be half an angel, but she's half a devil too." I'd say she was a fully-fledged devil.

Apart from the difficulties that can arise between parents and children, disagreements between husband and wife are also frequent, and at times they seriously upset family peace. What advice would you give to married couples in this respect?

I would advise them to love one another and to recognize   108
that although disagreements and difficulties will crop up throughout their lives, if they are solved with naturalness they can even contribute to deepening their love.

Each of us has his own character, his personal tastes, his moods—at times his bad moods—and his defects. But we all have likeable aspects in our personality as well, and for this reason, and many others, everyone can be loved. It is possible to live happily together when everyone tries to correct his own defects and makes an effort to overlook the faults of others. That is to say, when there is love which cancels out and overcomes everything that might seem to be a motive for coldness or disagreement. On the other hand, if husband and wife dramatize their little differences and reproach each other for their defects and mistakes, they put an end to peace and run the risk of killing their love.

Couples have the grace of the married state—the grace they receive in the sacrament of marriage—which enables them to live all the human and Christian virtues in their married life: understanding, good humor, patience, forgiveness, refinement, and consideration in their mutual relations. The important thing is not to give up the effort, not to give in to nerves, pride, or personal fads or obsessions. In order to achieve this, husband and wife must grow in interior life and learn from the Holy Family to live with refinement, for supernatural and at the same time human reasons, the virtues of a Christian home. I repeat again that the grace of God will not be lacking.

Anyone who says he cannot put up with this or that, or finds it impossible to hold his peace, is exaggerating in order to justify himself. We should ask God for the strength to overcome our whims and practice self-control. When we lose our temper we lose control of the situation. Words can become harsh and bitter, and we end up by offending, wounding, and hurting, even though we didn't mean to.

We should all learn to keep quiet, to wait and say things in a positive, optimistic way. When her husband loses his temper, the moment has arrived for the wife to be especially patient until he calms down, and vice versa. If there is true love and a real desire to deepen it, it will very rarely happen that the two give in to bad temper at the same time.

Another very important thing is to get used to the fact that we are never a hundred percent right. In fact, one can say that in matters like these, which are usually so debatable, the surer we are of being completely right, the more doubtful it is that we really are. Following this line of reasoning makes it easier to correct oneself later on and, if necessary, to beg pardon, which is the best way of ending a quarrel. In this way peace and love are regained. I am not encouraging you to quarrel, but it is understandable that we should fall out at times with those we love most, because they are the people we are always with. We are not going to fall out with someone in Timbuktu! Thus small rows between husband and wife, if they are not frequent (and they should see to it that they are not), are not a sign that love is missing, and in fact they can help to increase it.

Finally, I would advise parents never to quarrel in front of their children. They can remind each other of this with a certain word, a look, or a gesture. If they can't avoid the argument altogether, they can at least put it off till later, when they are more calm. The family atmosphere should be one of peace between husband and wife because it is a necessary condition for a deep and effective education. Children should see in their parents an example of dedication, sincere love, mutual help, and understanding. The small trifles of daily life should not be allowed to hide from them the reality of a love that is capable of overcoming all obstacles.

At times we take ourselves too seriously. All of us get angry now and again. Sometimes because it is necessary; at other times because we lack a spirit of mortification. The important thing is to show, with a smile that restores family warmth, that these outbursts of anger do not destroy affection.

In a word, the life of husband and wife should consist in loving one another and loving their children, because by doing this they love God.

A school run by the Women's Section of Opus Dei was opened recently in Madrid, with the aim of creating a family environment and offering a complete training program for domestic staff which will enable them to become qualified in their profession. What influence do you think these kinds of activities of Opus Dei can have in society?

The main aim of this apostolic work (and there are many   109
similar ones directed by members of Opus Dei who work together with other people who are not members of our Association) is to dignify the work of domestic staff in such a way that they can do their work with a scientific approach. I say "with a scientific approach" because housework should be carried out as a true profession.

We must not forget that there are people who have wanted to present this work as something humiliating, but it is not. No doubt, the conditions under which this work used to be done were humiliating, and sometimes they still are even today when domestic staff are subjected in their work to the whim of an arbitrary employer who does not guarantee their rights and who gives them low wages and no affection. Employers must be brought to respect an adequate work-contract with clear and precise guarantees in which the rights and duties of both parties are clearly established.

Apart from these legal guarantees the person who offers this service must be trained for the job, which means she must be professionally prepared. I said "service"—although the word is not popular these days, because any job that is well done is a wonderful service to society, and this is as true of domestic work as it is of the work of a professor or judge. The only work that is not a service is that of a person who works for his own self-interest.

Housework is something of primary importance. Besides, all work can have the same supernatural quality. There are no great or mean tasks. All are great if they are done with love. Those which are considered great become small when the Christian meaning of life is lost sight of. On the other hand, there are apparently small things that can in fact be very great because of their real effects.

As far as I am concerned, the work of one of my daughters in Opus Dei who works in domestic employment is just as important as that of one who has a title. In either case all I am concerned about is that the work they do should be a means and an occasion for personal sanctification and the sanctification of their neighbor. The importance depends on whether a woman in her own job and position in life is becoming more holy and fulfilling with greater love the mission she has received from God.

Before God all men have the same standing, whether they are university professors, shop-assistants, secretaries, laborers, or farmers. All souls are equal. Only at times the souls of simple and unaffected people are more beautiful; and certainly those who are more intimate with God the Father, God the Son, and God the Holy Spirit are always more pleasing to our Lord.

With this school that has been opened in Madrid a lot can be done. It can be a real and effective help to society in an important task; and a Christian work in the heart of the home, bringing happiness, peace, and understanding to many households. I could go on talking for hours on this subject, but what I have already said is enough to make clear that I understand that work in the home is specially important because through it so much good or harm can be done to families. Let us hope that it will do much good and that there will be many able and upright people whose apostolic zeal will draw them to turn this profession into a happy and fruitful task in so many homes throughout the world.

Many different factors, among which must be included the teaching of the Church's Magisterium, have contributed to create and promote the deep social awareness that exists today. We hear a lot about the virtue of poverty as giving witness to Christianity. How can a housewife, whose duty it is to secure the well-being of her family, live this virtue?

"The poor will have the gospel preached to them" (Mt 11:6) 110 we read in Scripture precisely as one of the signs which mark the arrival of the kingdom of God. Those who do not love and practice the virtue of poverty do not have Christ's spirit. This holds true for everyone. For the hermit who retires to the desert and for the ordinary Christian who lives among his fellow men, whether he enjoys the use of this world's resources or is short of many of them.

I would like to go into this topic at some length because when poverty is preached nowadays it is not always made clear how its message can be applied in daily life. There are some people, well-intentioned, no doubt, but they haven't quite managed to move with the times, who preach a poverty which is the result of "armchair speculation." This poverty has certain ostentatious outward signs, while at the same time it betrays enormous interior—and also sometimes exterior—deficiencies.

Recalling an expression of the prophet Isaiah—*discite benefacere* (1:17)—I like to say that we have to learn to live every virtue, and perhaps this is especially true of poverty. We have to learn to live it; otherwise it will be reduced to an ideal about which much is written but which no one seriously puts into practice. We have to make people see that poverty is an invitation which our Lord makes to each Christian, and that it is therefore a definite call that should shape every human life.

Poverty is not a state of miserable want; and it has nothing to do with dirtiness. Because, to start with, what makes a Christian is not so much the external conditions of his existence as the attitude of his heart. And with this, we are getting close to a very important point, on which a correct understanding of the lay vocation depends. For poverty is not simply renunciation. In certain circumstances Christians may be asked to give up everything as a testimony of poverty; they may be asked to challenge directly a society bent on material well-being and thus proclaim to the four winds that nothing is good if it is preferred to God. However, is this the witness that the Church usually asks today? Isn't it also asking us to give an explicit testimony of love for the world and of solidarity with our fellow men?

Sometimes when people consider Christian poverty they take as their main point of reference the religious whose job it is to give, at all times and in all places, official and public testimony of poverty. Such considerations run the risk of not recognizing the specific characteristics of a lay testimony, lived interiorly, in the ordinary circumstances of every day.

The ordinary Christian has to reconcile two aspects in his life that can at first sight seem contradictory. There is, on the one hand, true poverty, which is obvious and tangible and made up of definite things. This poverty should be an expression of faith in God and a sign that the heart is not satisfied with created things and aspires to the Creator; that it wants to be filled with love of God so as to be able to give this same love to everyone. On the other hand, an ordinary Christian is and wants to be one more among his fellow men, sharing their way of life, their joys and happiness; working with them, loving the world and all the good things that exist in it; using all created things to solve the problems of human life and to establish a spiritual and material environment which will foster personal and social development.

Achieving a synthesis between these two aspects is to a great extent a personal matter. It requires interior life, which will help us assess in every circumstance what God is asking of us. For this reason I do not want to give fixed rules, although I will give some general indications with special reference to mothers of families.

Poverty consists in large measure in sacrifice. It means   111
knowing how to do without the superfluous. And we find out what is superfluous not so much by theoretical rules as by that interior voice which tells us we are being led by selfishness or undue love of comfort. On the other hand, comfort has a positive side which is not luxury or pleasure-seeking but consists in making life agreeable for one's own family and for others so that everyone can serve God better.

Poverty lies in being truly detached from earthly things and in cheerfully accepting shortage or discomfort if they arise. Furthermore, it means having one's whole day taken up with a flexible schedule in which, besides the daily norms of piety, an important place should be given to rest, which we all need, to family get-togethers, to reading, and to time set aside for an artistic or literary hobby or any other worthwhile pastime. We live poverty by filling the hours of the day usefully, doing everything as well as we can, and living little details of order, punctuality, and good humor. In a word, it means finding opportunities for serving others and finding time for oneself without forgetting that all men, all women— not only those who are poor in a material sense—have an obligation to work. Wealth and abundance of economic means only increase one's obligation to feel responsible for the whole of society.

It is love that gives meaning to sacrifice. Every mother well knows what it means to sacrifice herself for her children; it is not a matter of giving them a few hours of her time but of spending her whole life in their benefit. We must live thinking of others and using things in such a way that there will be something to offer to others. All these are dimensions of poverty which guarantee an effective detachment.

It is not enough for a mother to live in this way. She should also teach her children to do so. She can do this by fostering in them faith, optimistic hope, and charity; by teaching them not to be selfish and to spend some of their time generously in the service of other less fortunate people, doing jobs suited to their age, in which they can show in a practical way a human and supernatural concern for their fellow men.

To sum up: each person has to go through life fulfilling his vocation. To my way of thinking, the best examples of poverty are those mothers and fathers of large and poor families who spend their lives for their children and who with their effort and constancy—often without complaining of their needs—bring up their family, creating a cheerful home in which everyone learns to love, to serve, and to work.

Throughout this interview you have commented on important aspects of human life, in particular those which refer to women, and on the value that is given to them in the spirit of Opus Dei. In conclusion, could you give us your opinion as to how the role of women in the life of the Church can best be promoted?

I must admit this question tempts me to go against my usual 112 practice and give instead a polemical answer, because the term *Church* is frequently used in a clerical sense as meaning *proper to the clergy or Church hierarchy.* And therefore many people understand participation in the life of the Church simply or at least principally as helping in the parish, cooperating in associations which have a mandate of the hierarchy, taking an active part in the liturgy, and so on.

Such people forget in practice, though they may proclaim it in theory, that the Church comprises all the People of God. All Christians go to make up the Church. Therefore, the Church is present wherever there is a Christian who strives to live in the name of Christ.

In saying this I am not seeking to minimize the importance of the role of women in the life of the Church. On the contrary, I consider it indispensable. I have spent my life defending the fullness of the Christian vocation of the laity, of ordinary men and women who live in the world, and I have tried to obtain full theological and legal recognition of their mission in the Church and in the world. I only want to point out that some people advocate an unjustifiable limitation of this collaboration. I must insist that ordinary Christians can carry out their specific mission—including their mission in the Church—only if they resist clericalization and carry on being secular and ordinary, that is, people who live in the world and take part in the affairs and interests of the world.

It is the task of the millions of Christian men and women who fill the earth to bring Christ into all human activities and to announce through their lives the fact that God loves and wants to save everyone. The best and most important way in which they can participate in the life of the Church, and indeed the way which all others presuppose, is by being truly Christian precisely where they are, in the place to which their human vocation has called them.

It is very moving to think of so many Christian men and women who, perhaps without any specific resolve, are living simple, ordinary lives and trying to make them a living embodiment of the will of God. There is an urgent need in the Church to make these people conscious of the sublime value of their lives, to reveal to them that what they are doing, unimportant though it appears, has an eternal value, to urge them, to teach them to listen more attentively to the voice of God, who speaks to them through everyday events and situations. God is urging the Church to fulfill this task, the task of making the entire world Christian from within, showing that Christ has redeemed all mankind. Women will participate in this task in the ways that are proper to them, both in the home and in other occupations which they carry out, developing their special characteristics to the full.

The main thing is that, like Mary, who was a woman, a virgin, and a mother, they live with their eyes on God, repeating her words, *Fiat mihi secundum verbum tuum* [be it done unto me according to thy word] (Lk 1:38). On these words depends the faithfulness to one's personal vocation—which is always unique and non-transferable in each case—which will make us all cooperators in the work of salvation which God carries out in us and in the entire world.

Passionately Loving the World

A homily given on October 8, 1967

You have just been listening to the solemn reading of the two texts of Sacred Scripture for the Mass of the twenty-first Sunday after Pentecost. Having heard the Word of God you are already in the right atmosphere for the words I want to address to you: words of a priest, spoken to a large family of the children of God in his Holy Church. Words, therefore, which are intended to be supernatural, proclaiming the greatness of God and his mercies toward men; words to prepare you for today's great celebration of the Eucharist on the campus of the University of Navarre.

Consider for a moment the event I have just described. We are celebrating the holy Eucharist, the sacramental sacrifice of the Body and Blood of our Lord, that mystery of faith which binds together all the mysteries of Christianity. We are celebrating, therefore, the most sacred and transcendent act which we, men and women, with God's grace can carry out in this life: receiving the Body and Blood of our Lord is, in a certain sense, like loosening our ties with earth and time, so as to be already with God in Heaven, where Christ himself will wipe the tears from our eyes and where there will be no more death, nor mourning, nor cries of distress, because the old world will have passed away.[1]

This profound and consoling truth, which theologians usually call the eschatological meaning of the Eucharist, could, however, be misunderstood. Indeed, this has happened whenever people have tried to present the Christian way of life as something exclusively *spiritual*—or better, spiritualistic—something reserved for *pure*, extraordinary

175

people who remain aloof from the contemptible things of this world, or at most tolerate them as something that the spirit just has to live alongside, while we are on this earth.

When people take this approach, churches become the setting *par excellence* of the Christian way of life. And being a Christian means going to church, taking part in sacred ceremonies, getting into an ecclesiastical mentality, in a special kind of *world*, considered the ante-chamber to Heaven, while the ordinary world follows its own separate course. In this case, Christian teaching and the life of grace would pass by, brushing very lightly against the turbulent advance of human history but never coming into proper contact with it.

On this October morning, as we prepare to enter upon the memorial of our Lord's Pasch, we *flatly reject* this deformed vision of Christianity. Reflect for a moment on the setting of our Eucharist, of our Act of Thanksgiving. We find ourselves in a unique temple; we might say that the nave is the University campus; the altarpiece, the University library; over there, the machinery for constructing new buildings; above us, the sky of Navarre. . . .

Surely this confirms in your minds, in a tangible and unforgettable way, the fact that everyday life is the true setting for your lives as Christians. Your daily encounter with Christ takes place where your fellow men, your yearnings, your work, and your affections are. It is in the midst of the most material things of the earth that we must sanctify ourselves, serving God and all mankind.

114   This I have been teaching all the time, using words from holy Scripture: the world is not evil, because it comes from the hands of God, because it is his creation, because Yahweh looked upon it and saw that it was good.[2] It is we ourselves, men and women, who make it evil and ugly with our sins and unfaithfulness. Don't doubt it, my children: any attempt to escape from the noble reality of daily life is, for you men

and women of the world, something opposed to the will of God.

On the contrary, you must realize now, more clearly than ever, that God is calling you to serve him *in and from* the ordinary, secular, and civil activities of human life. He waits for us everyday, in the laboratory, in the operating theatre, in the army barracks, in the university chair, in the factory, in the workshop, in the fields, in the home, and in all the immense panorama of work. Understand this well: there is *something* holy, something divine hidden in the most ordinary situations, and it is up to each one of you to discover it.

I often said to the university students and workers who were with me in the thirties that they had to know how to *materialize* their spiritual lives. I wanted to warn them of the temptation, so common then and now, to lead a kind of double life: on the one hand, an inner life, a life related to God; and on the other, as something separate and distinct, their professional, social, and family lives, made up of small earthly realities.

No, my children! We cannot lead a double life. We cannot have a split personality if we want to be Christians. There is only one life, made of flesh and spirit. And it is that life which has to become, in both body and soul, holy and filled with God: we discover the invisible God in the most visible and material things.

There is no other way, my daughters and sons: either we learn to find our Lord in ordinary, everyday life, or we shall never find him. That is why I tell you that our age needs to give back to matter and to the apparently trivial events of life their noble, original meaning. It needs to place them at the service of the kingdom of God; it needs to spiritualize them, turning them into a means and an occasion for a continuous meeting with Jesus Christ.

The genuine Christian approach—which professes the 115

resurrection of all flesh—has always quite logically opposed "dis-incarnation," without fear of being judged materialistic. We can, therefore, rightly speak of a *Christian materialism*, which is boldly opposed to those materialisms which are blind to the spirit.

What are the sacraments, which people in early times described as the footprints of the Incarnate Word, if not the clearest expression of this way which God has chosen in order to sanctify us and to lead us to Heaven? Don't you see that each sacrament is the love of God, with all its creative and redemptive power, given to us through the medium of material things? What is this Eucharist which we are about to celebrate if not the Adorable Body and Blood of our Redeemer, which is offered to us through the lowly matter of this world (wine and bread), through the elements of nature, cultivated by man, as the recent Ecumenical Council has reminded us.[3]

It is understandable, my children, that the Apostle should write: "All things are yours, you are Christ's and Christ is God's."[4] We have here an ascending movement which the Holy Spirit, poured into our hearts, wants to call forth in this world: upward from the earth to the glory of the Lord. And to make it clear that in such a movement everything is included, even what seems most commonplace, Saint Paul also wrote: "In eating, in drinking, do everything for God's glory."[5]

116   This doctrine of Sacred Scripture, as you know, is to be found in the very core of the spirit of Opus Dei. It should lead you to do your work perfectly, to love God and your fellow men by putting love in the little things of everyday life, and discovering that *divine something* which is hidden in small details. The lines of a Castilian poet are especially appropriate here: "Write slowly and with a careful hand, for doing things well is more important than doing them."[6]

I assure you, my children, that when a Christian carries

out with love the most insignificant everyday action, that action overflows with the transcendence of God. That is why I have told you so often, and hammered away at it, that the Christian vocation consists in making heroic verse out of the prose of each day. Heaven and earth seem to merge, my children, on the horizon. But where they really meet is in your hearts, when you sanctify your everyday lives. . . .

I have just said, sanctify your everyday lives. And with these words I refer to the whole program of your task as Christians. Stop dreaming. Leave behind false idealisms, fantasies, and what I usually call *mystical wishful thinking:** If only I hadn't married; if only I had a different job or qualification; if only I were in better health; if only I were younger; if only I were older. Instead, turn to the most material and immediate reality, which is where our Lord is: "Look at my hands and my feet," said the risen Jesus, "be assured that it is myself; touch me and see; a spirit has not flesh and bones, as you see that I have." [7]

Light is shed upon many aspects of the world in which you live, when you start from these truths. Take your activity as citizens, for instance. A man who knows that the world—and not just the Church—is the place where he finds Christ, loves that world. He endeavors to become properly trained, intellectually and professionally. He makes up his own mind, in full freedom, about the problems of the environment in which he moves, and he takes his own decisions in consequence. As the decisions of a Christian, they derive from personal reflection, which strives in all humility to grasp the will of God in both the unimportant and the important events of his life.

But it never occurs to such a Christian to think or say that   117

---

* A play on words between *ojalá* ("would that," "if only") and *hojalata* ("tin-plate"). *Mística ojalatera* is "tin-can mysticism," as well as "mystical wishful thinking."—Trans.

he was stepping down from the temple into the world to represent the Church, or that his solutions are *the Catholic solutions* to the problems. That would be completely inadmissible! That would be clericalism, *official Catholicism*, or whatever you want to call it. In any case, it means doing violence to the very nature of things. What you must do is foster a real *lay mentality*, which will lead to three conclusions: —be honorable enough to shoulder your own personal responsibility; —be Christian enough to respect those brothers in the faith who, in matters of free discussion, propose solutions that differ from yours; and —be Catholic enough not to make a tool of our Mother the Church, involving her in human factions.

It is obvious that, in this field as in all others, you would not be able to carry out this program of sanctifying your everyday life if you did not enjoy all the freedom that proceeds from your dignity as men and women created in the image of God and that the Church freely recognizes. Personal freedom is essential for the Christian life. But do not forget, my sons, that I always speak of a responsible freedom.

Interpret, then, my words as what they are: a call to exercise your rights every day, and not just in times of emergency. A call to fulfill honorably your commitments as citizens in all fields—in politics and in financial affairs, in university life and in your job—accepting with courage all the consequences of your free decisions and shouldering the personal independence that is yours. A Christian *lay outlook* of this sort will enable you to flee from all intolerance, from all fanaticism. To put it positively, it will help you live in peace with all your fellow citizens, and to promote understanding and harmony in the various spheres of social life.

118   I know I have no need to remind you of something which I have been saying for so many years. This doctrine of civic freedom, of understanding, of living in harmony with other

people, forms a very important part of the message spread by Opus Dei. Must I affirm once again that the men and women who want to serve Jesus Christ in the Work of God, are simply *citizens the same as everyone else*, who strive to live their Christian vocation to its ultimate consequences with a deep sense of responsibility?

Nothing distinguishes my children from their fellow citizens. On the other hand, apart from the faith they share, they have nothing in common with the members of religious congregations. I love the religious, and I venerate and admire their apostolates, their cloister, their separation from the world, their *contemptus mundi*, which are *other* signs of holiness in the Church. But the Lord has not given me a religious vocation, and for me to desire it would not be in order. No authority on earth can force me to be a religious, just as no authority can make me marry. I am a secular priest: a priest of Jesus Christ who is passionately in love with the world.

These are the men and women who have followed Jesus 119 Christ in the company of this poor sinner: a small percentage of priests, who have previously exercised a secular profession or trade; a large number of secular priests from many dioceses throughout the world, who in this way confirm their obedience to their respective bishops, their love for their diocesan work, and the effectiveness of it. Their arms are always wide open, in the form of a cross, to make room in their hearts for all souls; and like myself they live in the hustle and bustle of the workaday world which they love. And finally, a great multitude made up of men and women of different nations, and tongues, and races, who earn their living with their work. Most of them are married, many others single; they share with their fellow citizens in the important task of making temporal society more human and more just. And they work, as I have said, shoulder to shoulder with their fellow men, experiencing with them successes and failures in the noble struggle of daily endeavor, as they strive to fulfill their duties and to exercise their social and civic rights. And all this with naturalness, like any other conscientious Christian, without considering themselves special. Blended into the mass of their companions, they try at the same time to detect the flashes of divine splendor that shine through the commonest everyday realities.

Similarly, the activities that are promoted by Opus Dei as an association have these eminently secular characteristics: they are not ecclesiastical activities—they do not in any way represent the hierarchy of the Church. They are the fruit of human, cultural, and social initiatives of ordinary citizens who try to make them reflect the light of the gospel and to bring them the warmth of Christ's love. An example that will help to make this clear is that Opus Dei does not, and never will, undertake the task of directing diocesan seminaries, in which bishops *instituted by the Holy Spirit* [8] train their future priests.

120   Opus Dei, on the other hand, does foster technical training centers for industrial workers, agricultural training schools for farm laborers, centers for primary, secondary, and university education, and many other varied activities all over the world, because its apostolic zeal, as I wrote many years ago, is like a sea without shores.

But what need have I to speak at length on this topic, when your very presence here is more eloquent than a long address? You, Friends of the University of Navarre, are part of a body of people who know it is committed to the progress of the broader society to which it belongs. Your sincere encouragement, your prayers, sacrifices, and contributions are not offered on the basis of Catholic confessionalism. Your cooperation is a clear testimony of a well-formed social conscience, which is concerned with the temporal common good. You are witnesses to the fact that a university can be born of the energies of the people and be sustained by the people.

On this occasion, I want to offer my thanks once again for the cooperation lent to our University by my noble city of Pamplona, by the region of Navarre, by the Friends of the University from every part of Spain and—I say this with particular feeling—by people who are not Spaniards, even by people who are not Catholics or Christians, who have understood the purpose and spirit of this enterprise and have shown it with their active help.

Thanks to all of them this University has grown ever more effective as a focus of civic freedom, of intellectual training, of professional endeavor, and a stimulus for university education generally. Your generous sacrifice is part of the foundation of this whole undertaking, which seeks to promote the human sciences, social welfare, and the teaching of the faith.

What I have just pointed out has been clearly understood by the people of Navarre, who also recognize that their University is a factor in the economic development and, especially, in the social advancement of the region; a factor which has given so many of their children an opportunity to enter the intellectual professions that otherwise would have been difficult and, in some cases, impossible to obtain. This awareness of the role that the University would play in their lives is surely what inspired the support that Navarre has lent it from the beginning—support that will undoubtedly keep on growing in enthusiasm and extent.

I continue to harbor the hope—because it accords both   121
with the requirements of justice and with the practice that obtains in so many countries—that the time will come when the Spanish government will contribute its share to lighten the burden of an undertaking that seeks no private profit but, on the contrary, is totally dedicated to the service of society

and tries to work efficiently for the present and future prosperity of the nation.

And now, my sons and daughters, let me consider another aspect of everyday life that is particularly dear to me. I refer to human love, to the noble love between a man and a woman, to courtship and marriage. I want to say once again that this holy human love is not something to be merely permitted or tolerated alongside the true activities of the spirit, as might be insinuated by those false spiritualisms which I referred to earlier. I have been preaching and writing just the very opposite for forty years, and now those who did not understand are beginning to grasp the point.

Love, which leads to marriage and family, can also be a marvelous divine way, a vocation, a path for a complete dedication to our God. Do things perfectly, I have reminded you. Put love into the little duties of each day; discover that *divine something* contained in these details. All this teaching has a special place in that area of life where human love has its setting.

All of you who are lecturers or students or who work in any capacity in the University of Navarre know that I have entrusted your love to Mary, Mother of Fair Love. And here, on the University campus, you have the shrine, which we built so devoutly, as a place to receive your prayers and the offering of that wonderful and pure love on which she bestows her blessing.

"Surely you know that your bodies are the shrines of the Holy Spirit, who is God's gift to you, so that you are no longer your own masters?" [9] How often, before the statue of the Blessed Virgin, of the Mother of Fair Love, will you not reply to the Apostle's question with a joyful affirmation: Yes, we know that this is so and we want to live it with your powerful help, O Virgin Mother of God.

Contemplative prayer will rise within you whenever you

meditate on this impressive truth: something as material as my body has been chosen by the Holy Sprit as his dwelling place. . . . I no longer belong to myself. . . . My body and soul, my whole being, belong to God. . . . And this prayer will be rich in practical results arising from the great consequence which the Apostle himself suggests: "Glorify God in your bodies." [10]

Besides, you cannot fail to realize that only among those who understand and value in all its depth what we have just considered about human love can there arise another ineffable insight of which Jesus speaks:[11] an insight which is a pure gift of God, moving a person to surrender body and soul to the Lord, to offer him an undivided heart, without the mediation of earthly love. 122

I must finish now, my children. I said at the beginning that I wanted to tell you something of the greatness and mercy of God. I think I have done so in speaking to you about sanctifying your everyday life. A holy life in the midst of secular affairs, lived without fuss, with simplicity, with truthfulness: is this not today the most moving manifestation of the *magnalia Dei*,[12] of those prodigious mercies which God has always worked and still works, in order to save the world? 123

Now, with the Psalmist I ask you to join in my prayer and in my praise: *Magnificate Dominum mecum, et extollamus nomen eius simul* [13]—"Praise the Lord with me, let us extol his name together." In other words, my children, let us live by faith.

Let us take up the shield of faith, the helmet of salvation, and the sword of the Spirit, which is God's Word. That is what Saint Paul encourages us to do in the epistle to the Ephesians,[14] which was read in the liturgy a few moments ago.

Faith is a virtue which we Christians greatly need, and in a special way in this "Year of Faith," which our beloved Holy

Father Pope Paul VI has decreed. For, without faith, we lack the very foundation for the sanctification of ordinary life.

A living faith in these moments, because we are drawing near to the *mysterium fidei*,[15] to the Holy Eucharist: because we are about to participate in our Lord's Pasch, which sums up and effects the mercies of God toward men.

Faith, my children, in order to acknowledge that within a few moments *the work of our Redemption*[16] is going to be renewed on this altar. Faith, to savor the Creed and to experience, around this altar and in this assembly, the presence of Christ, who makes us *cor unum et anima una*,[17] "one heart and one soul," and transforms us into a family, a Church which is one, holy, catholic, apostolic, and Roman, which for us is the same as saying "universal."

Faith, finally, my beloved daughters and sons, to show the world that all this is not just ceremonies and words, but a divine reality, as we present to mankind the testimony of an ordinary life made holy, in the name of the Father and of the Son and of the Holy Spirit and of Holy Mary.

Notes

1. Freedom and Pluralism in the People of God

1. Schema of the Decree *Presbyterorum ordinis* (Vatican City: Typis Polyglottis Vaticanis, 1965), p. 68.
2. The Priestly Society of the Holy Cross is an Association which is proper and intrinsic to the Prelature and inseparable from it. It is made up of the clergy incardinated in Opus Dei and other priests or deacons incardinated in various dioceses. These priests and deacons of other dioceses—who do not form part of the Prelature's clergy but belong to the presbytery of their respective dioceses and depend exclusively on their Ordinary, as their Superior—associate themselves to the Priestly Society of the Holy Cross in order to seek their sanctification according to the spirit and ascetical praxis of Opus Dei. The Prelate of Opus Dei is concurrently President General of the Priestly Society of the Holy Cross.
3. We refer to all that was said in the Preface of this volume about some answers regarding aspects of law and organization, which were accurate and precise at the time when Opus Dei had not yet received the definitive juridical framework desired by its Founder: today they would have to be completed with the brief explanation given in the Preface.

2. Why Opus Dei?

1. J. Herranz, "The Evolution of the Secular Institute," in *Irish Ecclesiastical Record* (October-November 1965), pp. 249-277.
2. Monsignor Escrivá pointed out many times that Opus Dei was not de facto a Secular Institute, nor was it "a common association of the faithful." Although in 1947 Opus Dei was approved as a Secular Institute, as a juridical solution least inadequate for Opus Dei in the juridical norms then in force in the Church, Monsignor Escrivá had thought for many years back that the definitive juridical status of Opus Dei would be found among the secular structures of personal jurisdiction, as is the case with personal Prelatures.
3. These corporate works, of a straight apostolic character, are promoted—as Monsignor Escrivá points out—by members of Opus Dei together with other people. The Opus Dei Prelature, which assumes only the responsibility of providing doctrinal and spiritual orientation, owns neither the companies or the bodies owning them, nor the buildings or furniture belonging to them. The Opus Dei faithful who work in those undertakings do so with personal freedom and responsibility, in full conformity with the laws of the land, and having obtained from the authorities the

187

same recognition granted to
similar activities of other citizens.

3. The Apostolate of Opus Dei in Five Continents

1. *Anuario Pontifico* (1966), pp. 885, 1226.
2. See note no. 2 for chapter 2, above. The erection of Opus Dei as a personal Prelature has juridically reinforced the unity of Opus Dei, making it very clear that the entire Prelature—men and women, priests and laity, married and single—constitutes an organic and indivisible pastoral unit, which carries out its apostolates through both the Men's Section and the Women's Section, under the government and direction of the Prelate. The Prelate then, helped by his Vicars and his Councils, provides and ensures the fundamental unity of spirit and jurisdiction between both Sections.

Aside from this, the only change which would have to be made in this answer is merely terminological: instead of "Counselor" it would be "Regional Vicar." All that Monsignor Escrivá says about the spirit in which leadership is practiced in Opus Dei continues to be fully in force.

4. What Is the Attraction of Opus Dei?

1. See note 2 for chapter 3, above.

5. Opus Dei: Fostering the Search for Holiness

1. *Ecclesiam suam*, part 1.
2. Jn 12:32.
3. Jn 3:30.
4. Acts 1:1.
5. Mt 5:48.

6. See note 2 for chapter 3, above. Since the erection of Opus Dei as personal Prelature, instead of "President General" one has to say "Prelate": he is Opus Dei's own Ordinary, and is helped in the exercise of his work of government by his Vicars and Councils. The Prelate is elected by the General Congress of Opus Dei; this election requires the Pope's confirmation, as is the traditional canonical norm for jurisdictional prelates elected by a college.
7. Mt 10:24.
8. Monsignor Escrivá mentions in this answer the two ways in which secular priests can belong to Opus Dei: (a) priests coming from the ranks of the lay members of Opus Dei, who are called to Holy Orders by the Prelate: they are incardinated in the Prelature and constitute its clergy. They dedicate themselves basically, though not exclusively, to the pastoral attention of the faithful incorporated to Opus Dei. Together with these, they carry out the specific apostolate of spreading a deep awareness of the universal call to holiness and apostolate in all the environments of society (see also the Foreword); (b) the secular priests already incardinated in a diocese can also share the spiritual life of Opus Dei, as Monsignor Escrivá points out at the beginning of this answer, by associating themselves to the Priestly Society of the Holy Cross, which is intrinsically joined to the Prelature, and whose President General is the Opus Dei Prelate. See the Foreword, page 9, where a brief explanation of this priestly asso-

ciation is given in the precise
juridical terms that Monsignor
Escrivá was not in a position to
use when he granted this interview.

9. 1 Cor 3:22.
10. Jn 4:10.
11. 2 Cor 4:7.
12. Heb 13:8.

6. The University at the Service of Society

No notes.

7. Women in Social Life and in Church Life

1. See chapter 8, "Passionately
Loving the World," pages 175ff.

8. Passionately Loving the World

1. See Rev 21:4.
2. See Gen 1:7ff.
3. See Vatican Council II, Pastoral
Constitution *Gaudium et spes*,
no. 38.
4. 1 Cor 3:22-23.
5. 1 Cor 10:31.
6. A. Machado, *Poesías Completas*,
vol. 159: Proverbios y cantares,
24 (Madrid: Espasa Calpe, 1940):
Despacito, y buena letra:
el hacer las cosas bien
importa más que el hacerlas.
7. Lk 24:39.
8. Acts 20:28.
9. 1 Cor 6:19.
10. 1 Cor 6:20.
11. Mt 19:11.
12. Sir 18:4.
13. Ps 33:4.
14. Eph 6:11ff.
15. 1 Tim 3:9.
16. Prayer over the Offerings, Mass
of the Ninth Sunday after Pentecost.
17. Acts 4:32.

Index of Scripture References

Keyed to marginal numbers in this volume

OLD TESTAMENT

Genesis
1: 7ff.   114
1: 27   14
2: 15   10, 24, 55
5: 2   14
15: 1–6   96
35: 9–15   96

Exodus
20: 12   101

Deuteronomy
10: 17   40
32: 4   70

Chronicles
19: 7   40

Psalms
33: 4   123
42: 4   102

Song of Songs
8: 7   91

Wisdom
11: 25   112
13: 1ff.   70

Ecclesiastes
15: 14   104
18: 5   123
24: 24   85, 105
39: 21   70
39: 39   70

Isaiah
1: 17   110

Habakkuk
2: 4   67, 72, 92

NEW TESTAMENT

Matthew
5: 48   11, 55, 62
7: 20   81
10: 24   66
11: 5   110
11: 30   97
15: 4   101
15: 14   93
16: 4   59
18: 20   103
18: 23–35   113
19: 3–11   97
19: 4   14
19: 11   122
19: 12   92
23: 13   93

Luke
1: 38   112
6: 44   81
24: 39   116

John
3: 8   23, 31
3: 16–17   112
3: 30   59
4: 10   72
6: 38–40   1
12: 32   59
13: 34–35   98
15: 15   102

Acts of the Apostles
1: 1   62
1: 8   51

2: 32   51
4: 32   123
9: 1–25   4
10: 34   40
18: 1–3   89
18: 3   4
18: 24–28   89
20: 28   119

Romans
1: 17   67, 72, 92
1: 20   70
2: 11   40
8: 21   11, 14, 59
13: 10   62

1 Corinthians
3: 4–9   36
3: 22–23   70, 115
4: 3–6   31
6: 19   121
6: 20   121
7: 20   16
10: 31   115
12: 1–11   2
12: 4–11   67
16: 19   103

2 Corinthians
4: 7   72

Galatians
3: 11   67, 72, 92
3: 27–28   14
3: 26–28   87
4: 31   34, 98

Ephesians
5: 23   58
5: 32   91
6: 9   40
6: 10–17   113
6: 11ff.   123

Colossians
1: 24   58
3: 14   62
3: 25   40

1 Timothy
2: 4   32, 112
3: 9   123
4: 4   70
6: 20   1

2 Timothy
2: 3   45
3: 12   88

Hebrews
10: 38   67, 72, 92
11: 11–12   96
13: 8   72, 102
13: 14   11

1 Peter
1: 17   40
2: 10   1, 2, 45

Revelation
21: 4   113

Index of Topics

Keyed to marginal numbers in this volume (except as noted)

abnegation: involves struggle, 67, 122.

aggiornamento: 1, 26, 72, 100.

apostolate: mission of all Christians, 1, 9, 45; being instruments of God, 36, 58; and freedom, 12, 19; of priests and laity, 4, 69; lay apostolate, 9, 20, 21; of friendship and confidence, 62, 71; through one's work, 18, 31, 70, 109; in the home, 89, 91, 92, 102-104; and service, 51, 73, 90, 119, 120; Christian leaven, sanctification of the world, 56-60, 112.

association: right of association in the Church, 7, 8, 16; associations of students, 78.

apostolic celibacy: 45, 92, 122.

authority: freedom, 2, 11, 59; in the family, 100, 101.

Baptism: vocation to sanctity, 14, 20, 21, 24, 47, 58, 91.

catechesis: 2, 5, 27, 29, 67, 99.

Catholics: 29, 47, 58, 59, 113.

charity: understanding and living it, 35, 44, 60, 117; and sacrifice, 97, 101, 111; service to others, 96, 109; affection, 105-107; in one's work, 10, 75, 116; in one's apostolate, 62; and conjugal love, 91, 92, 95, 108, 121; and unity, 54; and freedom, 56, 85, 98; and justice, 29.

chastity: glorious affirmation of, 92, 121, 122; and human love, 91, 105, 107, 108, 121.

children: relations between parents and, 100, 101; formation of, 89, 97, 105, 108, 111; education in the faith, 102, 103; and birth control, 93-95; childless marriages, 96; vocation of, 92, 104, 121, 122.

Christian "materialism": 113-116, 121.

Church: and faithfulness, 1, 23, 72; Holy Spirit and, 2, 21, 23, 40; people of God, 17, 21, 119; all Christians are the Church, 2, 59, 112, 113; unity, 14, 43, 54, 57, 61, 67, 123; sanctity (baptismal vocation), 14, 20, 21, 24, 47, 58, 91; celibacy and matrimony, 92; catholicity, 6, 32, 42, 44, 71; ecumenism, 22, 27, 29, 46, 85; apostolate, sanctification of the world, 11, 26, 45, 66; obedience and freedom, 2, 11, 29, 59, 61; bishops and priests, 8, 16; priests and the laity, 4, 69; religious and the laity, 118; and mission of the laity, 9, 20, 21; women in the Church, 14, 87; freedom of the laity, 12, 38, 48, 90, 99, 117; public opinion in the Church, 2; serving the Church, 47, 60.

clericalism: 47, 59; Christian presence in the world, 66, 117; and freedom of the laity, 2, 12, 34, 65, 112; and priestly ministry, 4.

conscience: freedom of, 29, 44; formation of, 93, 95.

creation: work and, 10, 24.

Christian life: universal call to sanctity, 47, 55, 61, 62; in the middle of the world, 58, 60, 103,

107, 112-114, 116; in ordinary life, 11, 27, 87, 91, 121, 123; and freedom, 48, 99, 117; piety and interior life, 67, 70, 102, 115; Christian leaven as apostolate, 9, 18, 45, 51, 56, 57, 90; Christian "materialism," 113-116, 121.

Christian vocation: baptismal vocation, 14, 20, 21, 24, 47, 58, 91; supernatural, 64, 88, 104, 108; and sanctification of work, 10, 55, 60, 61; and apostolate, 9, 18, 20, 21, 31, 59, 70, 109; and freedom, 12, 27, 90, 117; and unity of life, 113-116.

culture: 73, 120.

divine filiation: and piety, 102, 103; and unity of life, 3.

doctrine: and Magisterium of the Church, 11, 29, 59; and formation, 2, 73; and piety, 102.

domestic help: 88, 109.

ecclesiastical hierarchy: Magisterium of the Church, 11, 29, 59; faithfulness to, 1, 23; obedience and freedom, 2, 29, 59, 61; unity with the hierarchy and freedom of Christians, 12, 112; right of association of priests, 7, 8, 16; mission of the laity in the Church, 20, 21.

ecumenism: 22, 27, 29, 44, 46, 85.

education, Christian: 73, 81, 84, 99, 102, 103; of children, 89, 100, 101, 108, 111; university, 73-76; education in freedom, 13, 84. *See also* university.

engagement: 105, 106, 121.

Eucharist, Blessed: 113-115, 123.

examination of conscience: 72.

faith: and Christian vocation, 1, 58, 95, 123; formation and piety, 73, 102.

family: path to sanctity, 91, 99,

112, 121; charity, authority, and freedom in, 98, 100, 101, 104; and the mother, 87, 88, 97, 107, 108; relationships between parents and children, 100, 101, 108; family piety, 102, 103; large families, 89, 94, 95, 111; spirit of poverty and of service, 110, 111.

faithfulness: 1; to the will of God, 32, 68; to the faith itself, 44, 62, 72, 90, 95; in the Church, 23.

first Christians: 24, 62, 89, 103.

formation: doctrinal, 2, 53, 73; of the conscience, 93; in the family, 89, 100, 101; and freedom, 63, 67, 74, 76, 77, 84, 99.

freedom: love for, 59, 66, 67, 74, 77; respect for, 30, 33, 34, 38, 50; responsible freedom, 29, 49, 52, 104, 116, 117; and charity, 56, 98; and obedience, 2, 11, 59; of consciences, 29, 35, 44, 63, 73, 85; of priests, 5, 7, 8; of the laity in the Church, 12, 20, 21; in the apostolate, 11, 19, 36; in matters of opinion, 28, 48, 65, 90, 108, 118; in teaching and education, 76, 79-81, 99; in the formation of children, 100, 101, 104.

friendship: 60, 90; with Jesus Christ, 102, 114, 116, 122; between parents and their children, 100, 101, 104; apostolate of, 62, 71.

generosity: and struggle, 67, 122; in marriage, 89, 94, 95.

glory of God: 115, 121, 123.

grace: 97, 108.

gospel: faithfulness to the gospel, 1, 28, 72; its message of sanctity, 24, 60, 62, 64; and of apostolate, 35, 57.

history, a sense of: 1, 72, 113.

Holy Spirit: his action in the

Church 2, 21, 23; his action in Christians, 31, 40, 55, 59, 67; and priests, 8; and supernatural life, 22, 115, 121.

home: path to sanctity, 91-93, 112, 121; relationships between parents and children, 100, 101, 108; charity, authority, and freedom in, 98, 104; family piety, 98, 103; work of the wife in the home, 87-89, 97, 107-109; spirit of poverty and service, 110, 111.

human dignity: love and respect for the freedom of others, 53, 66, 84, 117; dignity of human love, 105, 121, 122; of work, 10, 24, 55, 57, 109; of women, 14, 87, 90, 112; and formation, 73.

humility: knowledge of God and oneself, 72, 88; sacrifice and service to others, 96, 97, 108; collective, 40; integrist, 23, 44.

Jesus Christ: Redeemer and Supreme Priest, 1, 44; his call to sanctity and apostolate, 47, 62; the Christian as another Christ, 58, 60, 72, 88; following him in the middle of the world, 114, 116, 122; and sanctification of work, 10, 24, 55, 70; finding him in the center of all human activities, 59, 115; his love of freedom, 48, 98.

journalism: love and respect for freedom, 30, 50, 64, 86.

justice: love and respect for freedom, 29, 33; and service, 48, 75, 82, 83, 109, 120; in one's work 52, 109; and the spirit of poverty, 110, 111; and the common good, 73, 89.

laity: Christian vocation of, 58, 60, 61, 112, 116; their mission in the Church and in the world, 9, 14, 20, 21, 57, 59, 113; lay mentality,

117; sanctification of their work, 10, 18, 24, 26, 27, 56, 70, 16; specific apostolate of, 9, 11, 19-22; exercise of the virtues, 110, 111; priests and, 4, 69; religious and, 13, 54, 66, 118; freedom of, 12, 28, 34, 63-65, 90.

little things: sanctity and the insignificant, 115, 116, 121; presence of God in, 114; and charity, 107; and order, 88.

love of God: 105; and freedom, 104; and struggle, 67, 122; correspondence of one's life to, 10, 106, 116, 123; and the sacraments, 115; and the spirit of poverty, 110, 111.

love (human): 91, 92, 105-108, 121.

Magisterium of the Church: 47, 58, 93-95. *See also* ecclesiastical hierarchy.

marriage: divine vocation and path of sanctity, 45, 91-93, 112, 121; and conjugal love, 91, 107, 108, 121; faithfulness, 107; indissolubility, 1, 97; matrimonial formation, 92, 99; children and birth control, 89, 93-95, 111; relationships of parents with their children, 100, 101; family piety, 102, 103; childless marriages, 96; engagements, 105, 106, 121.

maturity: freedom, responsibility, and, 2, 104; criterion for, 93, 116; of the priest, 4; of women, 87; and formation of youths, 73-76.

"mystical wishful thinking": 88, 116.

obedience: and freedom 2, 11, 59. *See also* freedom.

Opus Dei:

—*corporate apostolate*: 18, 19, 27, 31, 41, 42, 51, 56, 82-84, 88,

109, 119, 120; with non-Catholics, 22, 27, 29, 44, 46.

—*formation*: 27, 29, 67, 99.

—*freedom and personal responsibility*: love and respect for freedom, 19, 27, 30, 38, 50, 66, 67, 117; freedom in personal matters, 28, 29, 48, 65, 118; freedom and charity, 31, 33, 56, 61, 98, 104.

—*government and organization*: 19, 35, 53, 63.

—*history*: 17, 24, 26, 30, 57, 72.

—*lay character*: apostolate of ordinary Christians, 22, 30, 34, 43, 49, 51, 52, 54, 60-62; baptismal vocation, 20, 21, 24, 58; love for the world, 26, 70, 72, 117, 119.

—*members* (faithful of the Prelature): 14, 40, 45, 56, 69, 119; citizens the same as others, 24, 26-28, 60, 61, 64-67, 118; priests, 4, 6, 16, 24, 69.

—*spirit and nature*: 24, 25, 70.

—*supernatural aim and means*: sanctity, 24, 26, 31, 55, 60-62, 67, 68, 112, 116; work, 10, 18, 24, 26, 27, 55-57; apostolate, 18, 41, 48, 51, 61, 84; of friendship and confidence, 27, 62, 71; marriage as a divinely ordained vocation, 45, 91, 92, 121; placing Christ at the center of human activities, 59, 70, 115.

—*supernatural character*: 30, 33, 39, 40, 54, 64-67; will of God and faith, 17, 32, 68, 114; universal call to sanctity, 24, 27, 31, 34, 56, 70, 121, 122; spirit of the first Christians, 24, 62; faithfulness and service to the Church, 16, 21, 29, 47, 59, 60.

—*universal character*: 32, 42; international scope, 18, 24, 31, 33, 37, 56, 71; in all areas of society, 18, 26, 40, 49, 56; and pluralism, 29, 30, 48, 49, 64, 98,

109, 119; unity and variety, 33, 35, 38, 67.

order: 88.

ordinary life: sanctity, 87, 91, 99, 112, 123; unity of Christian life, 113-116.

parental responsibility: 93-96; and large families, 89, 111.

patience: 100, 101, 108.

peace: 117.

personal prelature: pages 9-14; nos. 16, 19, 25, 35, 63, 69.

piety: 102, 103, 107; and unity of life, 113, 114.

plan of life: 111.

pluralism: and a love for freedom, 35, 67, 76; and respecting the freedom of others, 33, 38, 50, 98.

politics: and freedom, 77, 79; and service, 76, 90; and the priestly ministry, 5; and women in public life, 90.

poverty: cultivating a spirit of, 110, 111; and human means in the apostolate, 51, 83.

prayer: 70, 121; and piety 102; and priests as men of prayer, 3; in families, 103.

presence of God: 102, 103, 121; in one's work, 114, 116.

priesthood: mission of the priest, 4, 6, 47, 48, 69; sanctity and unity of life, 3, 16; unity with the hierarchy and freedom, 2, 8, 16; right of association, 7, 16; and preaching, 5; and spiritual direction, 93, and freedom of the laity, 12, 59, 61, 69.

Priestly Society of the Holy Cross: pages 13-14; nos. 16, 69.

public opinion: 50; in the Church, 2; and love and respect for human freedom, 30, 64, 86.

rectitude of intention: 31, 40, 93;

and love for the truth and freedom, 64, 66.

redemption: and God's universal saving will, 1, 32, 123; sanctification of the world, 10, 70, 91, 95, 112, 114; Christ at the center of human activities, 59, 115.

religious: love for, 43, 54; and the laity, 11, 13, 24, 62, 66, 110, 118.

responsibility: spiritual and personal formation, 74, 84, 93; responsible freedom, 29, 49, 52, 77, 90, 116, 117.

rest: 111.

Roman Pontiff: 22, 32, 46, 95.

sacraments: 9, 58, 91, 113, 115.

sacrifice: and charity, 91, 97, Ill.

sanctimoniousness: 102, 107.

sanctity: universal call to, 26, 34, 47, 55, 61, 62, 69; as following Christ in the middle of the world, 60, 113, 114, 116; in ordinary life, 87, 112, 123; in one's work, 10, 18, 24, 24, 27, 56, 70; in marriage, 25, 91–93, 112, 121; in personal and interior life, 31, 68, 99, 115.

Second Vatican Council: *see* Vatican Council II.

secular institutes: 24, 25.

secularity: 66, 113, 114, 116, 118.

serenity: 88, 100, 101, 108; and freedom, 56, 98, 118.

service: to society, 56, 74, 120; through one's work, 26, 27, 31, 55, 57, 109.

sin: 114.

sincerity: 102; and unity of life, 47, 107, 113, 114, 116.

solidarity: and freedom, 76, 84, 117; in one's work, 10, 75, 116; and the spirit of poverty, 110, 111.

spiritual direction: 93.

spiritualism: 113, 115.

totalitarianism: 33, 50, 99.

truthfulness: 33, 34, 41, 86; respect for, 64, 65.

understanding: 44, 98, 104, 108, 117; between parents and children, 101.

unity: 43, 43, 47, 54, 61; of the family, 98, 100, 101; and freedom, 67; and the Eucharist, 123; of life, 47; and piety, 102; sanctity, work, and apostolate, 62, 70; of priestly life, 3; and Christian materialism, 113–116, 121.

universality: 6, 32, 42, 64.

university education: service to society, 74-76, 82-84, 120; love for the truth, 73, 86; freedom and living in harmony together, 76-81, 85, 86

University of Navarre: 71, 82-84, 120.

Vatican Council II: fidelity to the Church 1, 23; on the universal call to sanctity, 47, 72; on priests, 3, 4; on the right of association by priests, 7, 8, 16; on the mission of the laity in the Church, 20, 21; on sanctification of work, 55; on marriage and family, 94; on Christian education, 81; on the apostolate of sanctification of the world, 11, 15, 26.

Virgin Mary: 87, 105, 112, 121.

virtues (supernatural and human): 62, 102, 108.

vocation: as involving struggle, 112, 121, 122.

will of God: and faithfulness, 17, 32, 68, 97; correspondence of one's life to, 92, 93, 106, 112, 114, 116.

women: mission in the church and society, 14, 112; role in the family, 87, 89, 97, 109; and professional vocations, 88, 90; and femininity, 87, 106, 107; the Virgin Mary and, 87, 112.

work: sanctification of, 10, 18, 24, 26, 27, 56, 116; of God, 24, 55, 57; and professional vocations as part of the Christian vocation, 60, 61, 64, 112; and personal and social worth, 31, 88, 109; professional competence and service, 68, 73, 75, 90; presence of God in, 114; and freedom, 12, 34; and the spirit of poverty, 110, 111; of women, 87-89, 109; and apostolate, 70, 71; and keeping Christ at the center of human activities, 59, 115.

world, the: love for, 70, 114, 116; Christian mission in the Church and in the world, 106, 112, 113, 115; freedom of Christians, 12, 28, 117; Christian ferment, 9, 18, 56, 57, 66; sanctification of the world, 11, 66, 72, 119, 120, 123; through work, 10, 24, 26, 27, 55, 116; professional vocations as part of the Christian vocation, 60, 61; sanctity of the family, 91, 94, 95, 97, 109; justice in, 48, 73, 89; and Christian "materialism," 113-116, 121; keeping Christ in the center of all human activities, 59, 115.

youths: freedom and responsibility, 104; and the ideal of service, 74, 75; life of piety, 102; relationships with parents, 100, 101; and human love, 92, 105, 106, 121, 122; youthful spirit of, 1, 102.

About the Author

Josemaría Escrivá de Balaguer was born in Barbastro, Spain, on January 9, 1902, the second of six children of Jose and Dolores Escrivá. Growing up in a devout family and attending Catholic schools, he learned the basic truths of the faith. Frequent confession and Communion, praying the Rosary, and almsgiving were a regular part of his childhood. The death of three younger sisters and his father's bankruptcy after business reverses taught him the meaning of suffering and brought maturity to his outgoing and cheerful temperament. In 1915, the family moved to Logroño, where his father had found new employment.

Beginning in 1918, Josemaría sensed that God was asking something of him. In order to be available for whatever God wanted of him, he began to study for the priesthood, first in Logroño and later in Saragossa. He was ordained a priest and began his pastoral ministry in 1925.

In 1927, Fr. Josemaría moved to Madrid to study for a graduate degree in law. He was accompanied by his mother, sister, and brother, as his father had died in 1924, and he was now head of the family. They were not well-off, and to support them he tutored law students. At the same time, he was active in pastoral work, especially among the poor and sick and with young children. To this work he enlisted manual workers, professional people, and university students so that they might learn the practical meaning of charity and their Christian responsibility to society.

On October 2, 1928, while making a retreat in Madrid, he understood his specific mission: he was to establish an institution within the Church dedicated to helping people in all walks of life to follow Christ, to seek holiness in their daily life, and to grow in love for God and their fellow men and women. This was the beginning of Opus Dei. He then dedicated all his strength to fulfilling this mission, certain that God had raised up Opus Dei to serve the Church. In 1930, he started Opus Dei's apostolic work with women, making clear that they had the same responsibility as men to serve society and the Church.

In 1934, he saw published his first collection of short points for prayer and reflection, under the title *Spiritual Considerations* (later translated into English as *The Way*). Expanded and revised, it has gone through many editions; more than four million copies in many different languages are now in print. His other spiritual writings include *Holy Rosary*; *The Way of the Cross*; two collections of homilies, *Christ Is Passing By* and *Friends of God*; and *Furrow* and *The Forge*, which, like *The Way*, are books for prayer and reflection.

The development of Opus Dei began among young people. Its growth, however, was seriously impeded by the religious persecution and other hardships inflicted on the Catholic Church during the Spanish Civil War (1936-1939). Fr. Josemaría himself suffered severe hardships under this persecution. After the war, he traveled throughout Spain giving retreats to priests at the request of their bishops. Opus Dei gradually spread from Madrid to several other Spanish cities, and when World War II ended, in 1945, it took root also in other countries. Although the Work always had the approval of the local bishops, its then-unfamiliar message of personal holiness in the world met with some misunderstandings and suspicions—which Fr. Escrivá bore with great patience and charity.

While celebrating Mass in 1943, he received a new foundational grace to establish the Priestly Society of the Holy Cross, making it possible for some of Opus Dei's laymen to be ordained as priests. The full incorporation of both lay faithful and priests in Opus Dei, which makes a seamless cooperation in the apostolic work possible, is an essential feature of the foundational charism of Opus Dei, affirmed by the Church in granting Opus Dei the canonical status of a personal Prelature. In addition, the Priestly Society conducts activities, with the approval of the local bishops, for the spiritual development of diocesan priests and seminarians. Diocesan priests can also be part of the Priestly Society.

Aware that God meant Opus Dei to be part of the mission of the universal Church, Fr. Escrivá moved to Rome in 1946. By 1950, the Work had received pontifical approvals affirming its main foundational features—spreading the message of holiness in daily life; service to the Pope, the universal Church, and the particular churches; secularity and naturalness; fostering personal freedom and responsibility; and a pluralism consistent with Catholic moral, political, and social teachings.

In 1948, full membership in Opus Dei was opened to married people. Two years later, the Holy See approved the idea of accepting non-Catholics and even non-Christians as cooperators in the Work—persons who assist Opus Dei in its projects and programs without becoming members. The next decade saw Opus Dei launching a wide range of undertakings of manifestly Christian inspiration: professional schools, agricultural training centers, universities, primary and secondary schools, and hospitals and clinics, open to people of all races, religions, and social backgrounds.

During Vatican Council II (1962–1965), now-Monsignor Escrivá worked closely with many of the Council fathers, discussing such themes as the universal call to holiness and the importance of the laity in the mission of the Church. He did everything possible to implement the Council's teachings in the formative activities offered by Opus Dei throughout the world.

Between 1970 and 1975, Monsignor Escrivá undertook catechetical trips throughout Europe and Latin America, speaking about love of God, the sacraments, Christian dedication, and the need to sanctify work and family life. By the time of his death, Opus Dei had spread to thirty nations on six continents. Now it has members in sixty countries, and their numbers have increased to more than 84,000.

Monsignor Escrivá's death in Rome came suddenly on June 26, 1975, at age 73. Large numbers of bishops and ordinary faithful petitioned the Vatican to begin the process of investigating the sanctity of this remarkable priest. On May 17, 1992, Pope John Paul II declared him Blessed before a huge crowd in St. Peter's Square. The date of his canonization—the Church's formal declaration that Josemaría Escrivá is a saint—is October 6, 2002.

—